EMERGENCY FIRST RESPONSE®

EMERGENCY
first response®

This Participant Manual belongs to _____

Mailing Address _____

City _____ State/Province _____

Zip/Postal Code _____ Country _____

Phone Number _____

Instructor Statement

This person has completed the Emergency First Response CPR & AED course requirements.

Instructor Signature _____ Number _____

Completion Date _____

Emergency First Response® (EFR®)
CPR & AED Participant Manual

© Emergency First Response Corp. 2017

No part of this product may be reproduced, sold or distributed in any form without the written permission of the publisher.
® indicates a trademark is registered in the U.S. and certain other countries.

Published by Emergency First Response Corp.
30151 Tomas, Rancho Santa Margarita, CA 92688-2125 USA

Printed in USA

ISBN 978-1-61381-992-0

Product No. 70185 (Rev. 03/17) Version 1.01

ACKNOWLEDGMENTS

For More Information

For more information about Emergency First Response Corp., courses, products and emergency care go to www.emergencyfirstresponse.com.

Patient Care Standards

Emergency First Response CPR & AED courses follow the emergency considerations and protocols as developed by the members of the International Liaison Committee on Resuscitation (ILCOR). Members include American Heart Association (AHA), European Resuscitation Council (ERC), Australian and New Zealand Committee on Resuscitation (ANZCOR—current members include Australian Resuscitation Council and New Zealand Resuscitation Council), Heart and Stroke Foundation of Canada (HSFC), Resuscitation Council of Southern Africa (RCSA), Inter American Heart Foundation (IAHF), Resuscitation Council of Asia (RCA – current members include Japan, Korea, Singapore, Taiwan, Philippine, Thai).

Source authority for the development of content material in Emergency First Response programs is based on the following:

- Circulation, Journal of the American Heart Association. Volume 122, Number 18, Supplement 3. November 2010, and Volume 132, Number 18, Supplement 2. November 2015. http://circ.ahajournals.org/content/vol132/18_suppl_2/ and https://eccguidelines.heart.org/index.php/circulation/cpr-ecc-guidelines-2/

- Resuscitation, Journal of the European Resuscitation Council. Volume 95, October 2015. http://www.resuscitationjournal.com/

- Australian Resuscitation Council and ARC, ANZCOR and ARC Guidelines, Version: January 2016. http://www.resus.org.au/guidelines/anzcor-guidelines/

- New Zealand Resuscitation Council Guidelines, ANZCOR and NZRC Guidelines, Version: January 2016. http://www.anzcor.org/guidelines/.

Emergency First Response gratefully acknowledges the following contributors for their assistance with publishing this manual:

International Medical Review

Dr.PhilBryson, MBChB, DCH, DRCOG, MRCGP
Medical Director of Diving Services
Abermed Ltd, Aberdeen

DesGorman, BSc, MB, ChB, FACOM, FAFOM, PhD, Dip DHM
Head - Occupational Medicine
School of Medicine, University of Auckland
Auckland, New Zealand

TonyKemp, MA DIMC RCSEd RN MAcadMEd
Vice-chairman & Director - BASICS Education Ltd
British Association for Immediate Care (BASICS), UK.

JanRisberg, MD, PhD
Bergen, Norway

BrianSmith, MD
Mountain West Anesthesia
Utah, USA

Equipment

Medtronic

PhillipsMedical Systems

The CardiacScience Corporation

ZollMedical Corporation

Table of **Contents**

Getting Started

Section One – Independent Study

Section Two – Skills Workbook

Introduction

In the company gym, an older gentleman complains of chest pain and an uncomfortable pressure and pain in his chest. A coworker unloading his truck suddenly collapses to the ground. An infant is found in her crib, unresponsive and not breathing normally. These things happen every day to coworkers, family members or people you meet on the street. Some of them just need a helping hand, while others will die or suffer permanent injury without immediate attention.

In an emergency, many variables separate those who escape serious disability or death from those who suffer long after their misfortune, or die. Individual fitness and health, the severity of the initial incident, the distance from medical care and often, just plain luck may make the difference. You can't control these variables, nor should you expect to. But, you can control one variable when you're on the scene of any medical emergency – you. Often, a layperson providing emergency care tips the balance in favor of life versus death, or complete recovery versus long-term disability. If you're there, you can provide that care. No, you can't guarantee that a patient will live or fully recover – there's too much beyond your control. But, given the circumstances, you can see to it that everything that could be done will be done. You can give the patient the best chances possible. In an emergency, what do you do? For that matter, how do you know what to do first? Although these questions may appear overwhelming, actually they're not. This is because no matter what the nature of a medical emergency – whether someone falls from a ladder or suffers from respiratory failure (such as after exposure to toxic fumes) causing cardiac arrest – you follow the same steps in the same order.

In the Emergency First Response® CPR & AED course, you'll learn the necessary emergency care steps in the right order, so you do the right things at the right time. You'll learn to apply emergency care following the same priorities used by medical professionals. The skills you'll learn apply specifically to CPR (Cardiopulmonary Resuscitation) and AED (Automatic External Defibrillator) use. These are skills that you can use to help others in need no matter where you are.

Who May Enroll in this Course and What Are the Prerequisites?

Anyone of any age may enroll in the Emergency First Response CPR & AED course. The course is performance-based, meaning that as long as you can meet each of the stated objectives and complete the necessary skills to the satisfaction of your instructor, you may receive a course completion card.

Emergency First Response **Courses**

Emergency First Response (EFR) is an international CPR, AED and first aid training organization. With more than 57,000 instructors, Emergency First Response is backed by 50 years of experience in the development and delivery of instructional courses, training materials and educational curricula.

Emergency First Response CPR & AED courses follow the emergency considerations and protocols as developed by the members of the International Liaison Committee on Resuscitation (ILCOR). Members include American Heart Association (AHA), European Resuscitation Council (ERC), Australian and New Zealand Committee on Resuscitation (ANZCOR—current members include Australian Resuscitation Council and New Zealand Resuscitation Council), Heart and Stroke Foundation of Canada (HSFC), Resuscitation Council of Southern Africa (RCSA), Inter American Heart Foundation (IAHF), Resuscitation Council of Asia (RCA – current members include Japan, Korea, Singapore, Taiwan, Philippine, Thai).

Focused on training lay emergency responders like you, the EFR instructional approach will build your confidence increasing your willingness to respond when faced with real medical emergencies. In all EFR courses, you will initially learn, practice and refine your emergency care skills in a relaxed environment.

To become the best Emergency Responder you can be, you are encouraged to take all EFR course offerings. Besides this course, other EFR courses include:

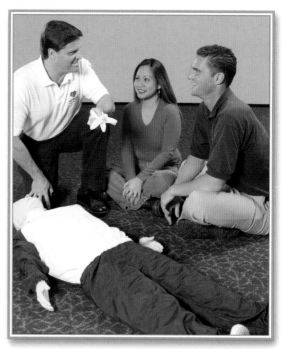

With more than 57,000 instructors, Emergency First Response is backed by 50 years of experience in the development and delivery of instructional courses, training materials and educational curricula.

Primary Care (CPR)

Emergency First Response Primary Care (CPR) teaches you the steps and techniques for handling life-threatening emergencies.

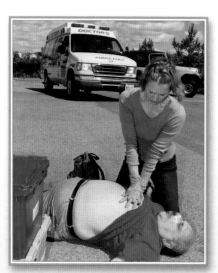

In it, you'll learn nine skills for aiding patients who aren't breathing normally, have no heartbeat, may have a spinal injury, may be in shock or who may have serious bleeding. You'll learn how to apply the *Cycle of Care*, so that you provide the patient with every possible chance of survival in the face of the most serious emergencies.

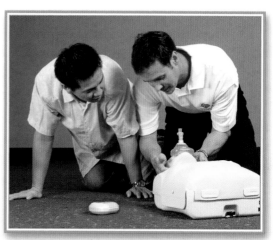

In all EFR courses, you will initially learn, practice and refine your emergency care skills in a relaxed environment.

Skills Taught in this Course:

▶ Scene Assessment

▶ Barrier Use

▶ Primary Assessment

▶ CPR – Chest Compressions

▶ CPR – Chest Compressions Combined
  With Rescue Breathing

▶ Optional Skill – Automated External
  Defibrillator Use

▶ Serious Bleeding Management

▶ Shock Management

▶ Spinal Injury Management

▶ Conscious/Unconscious Choking Adult

▶ Optional Skill – Emergency Oxygen Use Orientation

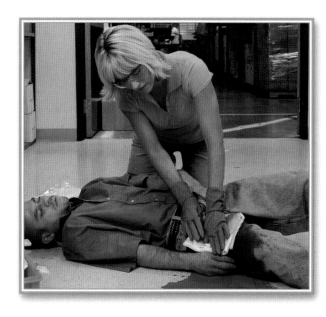

Secondary Care (First Aid)

Emergency First Response Secondary Care (First Aid) teaches you what to do when Emergency Medical Services (EMS) are either delayed or unavailable. This course also teaches you how to provide first aid for patients with conditions that aren't life-threatening. You'll learn to apply the *Cycle of Care* in such a way as to reduce imminent threats to a patient's life while providing care that reassures, eases pain and reduces the risk of further harm.

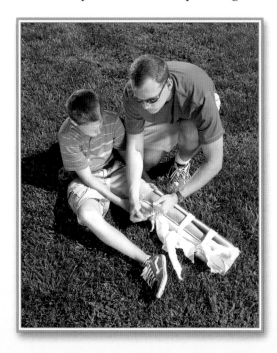

Skills Taught in this Course:

▶ Injury Assessment

▶ Illness Assessment

▶ Bandaging

▶ Splinting for Dislocations and Fractures

Care for Children

The Emergency First Response Care for Children course is an innovative CPR, AED and first aid training course that teaches participants how to provide emergency care for injured or ill children (age one year to puberty) and infants less than one year old. In this course you learn about the types of medical emergencies that children face, and how they differ from adult conditions. The curriculum also includes the importance of attending to basic emergency situations with children, the emotional aspects of caring for children, secondary care for children, and preventing common injuries and illnesses in children.

Emergency First Response Care for Children course trains the lay rescuer to follow the same priorities of care used by medical professionals. The course includes both primary care (CPR) and secondary care (first aid) skills. The primary care portion of the course prepares the rescuer to render aid to an infant or child with a life-threatening emergency such as choking or cardiac arrest. Secondary care focuses on developing secondary patient care skills and building the rescuer's confidence to render first aid to an infant or child in need when EMS is either delayed or unavailable.

Skills Taught in this Course:

- ▶ Scene Assessment and Barrier Use
- ▶ Primary Assessment
- ▶ Child CPR
- ▶ Optional Skill – AED Use with Children
- ▶ Infant CPR
- ▶ Conscious Choking Child
- ▶ Conscious Choking Infant

- ▶ Serious Bleeding Management
- ▶ Shock Management
- ▶ Spinal Injury Management
- ▶ Injury Assessment
- ▶ Bandaging
- ▶ Illness Assessment

First Aid at Work

These regionally specific EFR courses are specially designed for those individuals needing to meet government or corporate requirements to secure Emergency Responder credentials for the workplace. For more information ask your Instructor or contact your Emergency First Response Regional Headquarters listed at the front of this manual.

Keeping Your Skills Fresh

When you complete this course, make it a point to practice the included skills in this course from time to time. When not used or practiced, all skills deteriorate over time. Research proves that Emergency Responder skills can begin to deteriorate as soon as six months after initial training.

Hopefully, you won't have to use your emergency skills in an actual situation. But even if you don't, you still need to practice to keep your skills fresh and properly sequenced. Everyone is nervous when they arrive on the scene of badly injured or seriously ill individuals. Practicing your skills and keeping them fresh in your mind will reduce your nervousness and help you act appropriately. You can review and practice your skills on your own by:

- ▶ Reviewing your EFR Video.

- ▶ Re-reading this manual.

- ▶ Role-playing scenarios with your family members or friends.

- ▶ Walking through the CPR sequence using a pillow or appropriately-sized stuffed bag.

- ▶ Taking another EFR course. Consider refreshing your skills annually by taking another EFR course or an official EFR refresher course. As mentioned, there are five EFR courses you can take. All EFR courses use the same emergency care protocols, so by taking another course you upgrade your abilities while at the same time refreshing your previously acquired skills.

An easy and effective way to practice and fine-tune your emergency care skills is by enrolling in an Emergency First Response Refresher course.

About this **Manual**

The *Emergency First Response CPR & AED Participant Manual* has two sections

▶ **Section One – Independent Study Workbook**

▶ **Section Two – Skills Workbook**

Section One provides you with foundational information specific to Emergency Responder care. By reading the background information in this section, you'll better understand emergency care procedures and why your role as an Emergency Responder is so important to those who need emergency care.

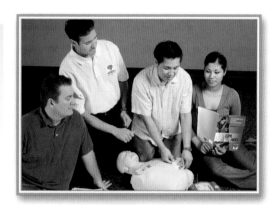

Section Two applies to the skill development portion of your CPR & AED course. Under the supervision of your Emergency First Response Instructor, you'll use this step-by-step workbook to guide you through the skill practice sessions. Depending on your personal needs and the need for your instructor to meet regional requirements for requisite skills, your instructor will include some or all of the nine skills in your course. This section will also involve real life scenarios you'll use to further refine your skills.

Regional Resuscitation Councils and Organizations

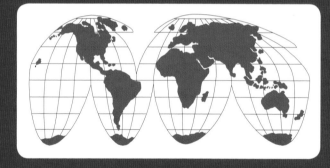

Within this manual, significant regional differences in CPR protocols and AED use are indicated by references to AHA, ERC or ANZCOR and ARC/NZRC guidelines.

◆ American Heart Association (AHA) guidelines are used in the Americas, United States, Canada, Asia and the Pacific Island countries.

◆ European Resuscitation Council (ERC) guidelines are used in Europe, the Middle East and Africa. Europe includes Eastern Europe and Russia.

◆ Australia and New Zealand Resuscitation Council (ANZCOR) and ARC/NZRC) guidelines are used in Australia and New Zealand.

Regional differences in emergency care protocols reflect local medical practice. These differences do not imply higher or lower standards of care as all protocols are based on the same source evidence.

Course **Structure**

This manual and the *Emergency First Response CPR & AED Video* are the study tools for the course. The nine skills outlined in this manual are:

- Scene Assessment
- Primary Assessment
- Adult CPR – Chest Compressions
- Adult CPR – Chest Compressions Combined With Rescue Breaths
- Adult CPR and AED Use

- Child CPR and AED Use
- Infant CPR
- Adult and Child Choking
- Infant Choking

Before attending your course, begin by reading the Independent Study section of this manual. Also, watch the *Emergency First Response CPR & AED Video*. Your instructor will guide you as to which skills you'll be learning in your regionally customized course.

Both learning tools – manual and video – provide you with important background information needed to understand why each topic and skill is important and how to perform the skills. When you attend the Skill Development and Scenario Practice session organized by your EFR Instructor you'll be capable and comfortable learning the required skills.

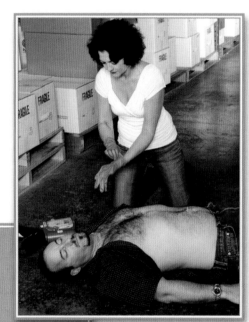

After you've practiced the skills in your course, your instructor will stage mock emergencies for you and your classmates. During these scenarios, you'll apply your skills and learn to adapt what you've learned to circumstances such as you might find in real life. This emphasis on practicing and adapting the required skills will allow you to be comfortable using them should an actual emergency occur.

Emergency First Response CPR & AED teaches you the steps and techniques for handling life-threatening emergencies.

Course **Flow**

Read the Independent Study portion of this Participant Manual.

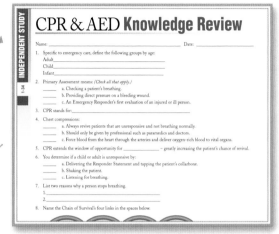

Complete the Knowledge Review at the end of the independent study portion of your Participant Manual.

Watch your *Emergency First Response Video.*

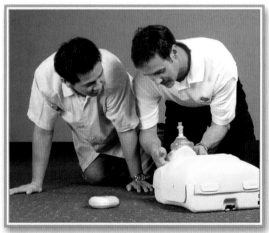

Attend the Skill Development session organized by your Emergency First Response Instructor.

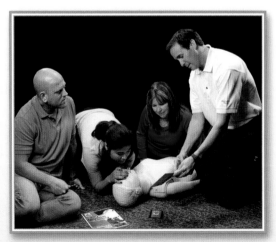

Complete the Scenario Practice with your Emergency First Response Instructor.

Learning **Tips**

Here are a few pointers to help you get the most out of the Emergency First Response CPR & AED course.

1. **Don't focus on perfection.** A common misconception with emergency care is that the smallest error will hurt or kill a patient. This is seldom true. Your instructor will make sure you understand what's critical and what's not. When someone focuses on perfection, there's a tendency to do nothing in a real emergency because that person fears not doing everything "perfectly." Don't get caught in that trap – it's not hard to provide adequate care. Always remember – *adequate care provided is better than perfect care withheld*.

2. **Don't be intimidated.** You're learning something new, so don't be surprised if you're not immediately comfortable with a skill or need some guidance. So what? If you already knew how to do it, you wouldn't be there. Mistakes aren't a problem – they're an important part of learning.

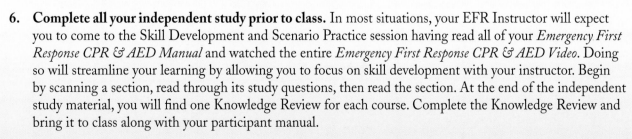

3. **Have fun.** That may sound odd given the seriousness of what you're learning, but the truth is, you'll learn more and learn faster if you and your classmates keep things light. Polite humor and light jests are normal in this kind of learning. But, be sensitive and aware that others taking the course with you may have been involved in a situation similar to what you're practicing. You can have fun without seeming insensitive or uncaring about human suffering.

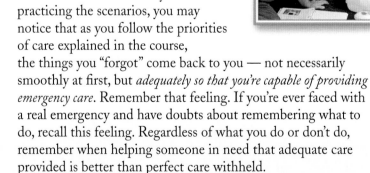

4. **Be decisive and then act.** There's more than one way to help a person that is injured or ill. When you practice the scenarios, you'll find that circumstances don't always give you clear direction in exactly how to best apply the priorities of care.

5. **It all comes back.** When you're practicing the scenarios, you may notice that as you follow the priorities of care explained in the course, the things you "forgot" come back to you — not necessarily smoothly at first, but *adequately so that you're capable of providing emergency care*. Remember that feeling. If you're ever faced with a real emergency and have doubts about remembering what to do, recall this feeling. Regardless of what you do or don't do, remember when helping someone in need that adequate care provided is better than perfect care withheld.

6. **Complete all your independent study prior to class.** In most situations, your EFR Instructor will expect you to come to the Skill Development and Scenario Practice session having read all of your *Emergency First Response CPR & AED Manual* and watched the entire *Emergency First Response CPR & AED Video*. Doing so will streamline your learning by allowing you to focus on skill development with your instructor. Begin by scanning a section, read through its study questions, then read the section. At the end of the independent study material, you will find one Knowledge Review for each course. Complete the Knowledge Review and bring it to class along with your participant manual.

Emergency Care Definitions and Background Information

Emergency First Response courses are skill intensive. However, skills alone are not enough. Knowing how, why and when to apply your skills during an emergency is important as well. The definitions and background information outlined here will give you the confidence to use your skills – knowing you are giving the correct care in the correct sequence.

Infant

Child

Emergency Care Age Definitions

Providing specific emergency care for a patient is in part guided by the age of the individual. For this reason, the emergency care outlined in this course is divided into adult, child and infant. Adults are defined as individuals typically older than 12 years (past puberty). Children are defined as individuals between the ages of 1 and 12 years old, but who not yet reached puberty. Infants are defined as individuals younger than 1 year. When actually delivering emergency care, if you are in doubt as to whether a patient is an adult or child, treat the patient as an adult.

Study Questions

- ◆ When giving emergency care, what are the age definitions for adult, child and infant?
- ◆ What is Primary Assessment?
- ◆ What does CPR stand for, what is it and how does it work?
- ◆ What do *unresponsive* and *not breathing normally* mean?
- ◆ How do you determine if a person is unresponsive and not breathing normally?
- ◆ What causes a person to stop breathing?
- ◆ How does rescue breathing work?

Primary Assessment

Primary means first in a series or sequence. It means most important. An assessment is an evaluation or an appraisal. Therefore, in terms of emergency care, a primary assessment is an Emergency Responder's first evaluation of an injured or ill person. Primary assessment is always the first step of any emergency care. Primary assessment also refers to the evaluation of a patient for any life-threatening conditions needing immediate attention. Injuries and illnesses that are life-threatening need to be treated first.

A primary assessment is an Emergency Responder's first evaluation of an injured or ill person.

CPR

CPR stands for Cardiopulmonary Resuscitation. Cardio means "heart" and Pulmonary means "concerning the lungs and breathing." Resuscitation means "to revive from unconsciousness." If a patient is unresponsive and not breathing normally, you begin CPR immediately.

CPR is a two-step process. First, and most important, you press on a patient's chest. These are called *chest compressions*. Second, you blow in the patient's mouth providing him oxygen. These are called *rescue breaths*. Rescue breaths can be delivered by mouth-to-mouth or mouth-to-mask. On young children and infants, rescue breaths can be delivered by sealing your lips tightly around the mouth and the nose. Complete CPR combines manual chest compressions with rescue breathing.

CPR is a two-step process. First, press on a patient's chest.

Second, blow in the patient's mouth.

C = CARDIO
"heart"

P = PULMONARY
"concerning the lungs – breathing"

R = RESUSCITATION
"to revive from unconsciousness"

How does CPR Work

The heart pumps oxygen-rich blood throughout the body. It also returns the oxygen-poor blood to the lungs for more oxygen. If a patient's heart has stopped, rescue breaths alone are ineffective. If a patient's heart has stopped, you must substitute manual chest compressions for the heart's pumping action to circulate blood through the body.

Chest compressions manually forces blood from the heart through the arteries and deliver oxygen-rich blood to vital organs. These manual chest compressions deliver no more than one third of normal blood flow to the body. Therefore, as an Emergency Responder you must begin compressions immediately and minimize interruptions during CPR. Delaying chest compressions for any reason is counterproductive. CPR is used as an interim emergency care procedure until the heart's normal rhythm is restored or more advanced care can be given.

CPR extends the window of opportunity for resuscitation – increasing the patient's chance of revival. That said, CPR rescue efforts are difficult to sustain for long periods and is exhausting. This is another reason to call for professional help (Emergency Medical Services – EMS) immediately. To reduce fatigue, change rescuers every few minutes. Switching rescuers will reduce deterioration of chest compression quality.

Regarding CPR, if you are unable or feel uncomfortable giving a nonbreathing patient rescue breaths – RELAX! Simply give the patient continuous chest compressions without rescue breaths. Chest compressions alone are very beneficial to a patient who is unresponsive and not breathing normally. Your efforts will still help circulate blood that contains some oxygen. Remember: *Adequate care provided is better than perfect care withheld.* You will learn adult, child and infant CPR during your Skill Development sessions.

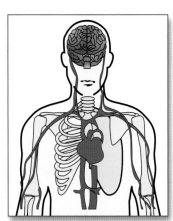

The heart pumps oxygen-rich blood throughout the body. It also returns the oxygen-poor blood to the lungs for more oxygen.

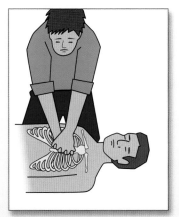

Chest compressions manually force blood from the heart through the arteries and deliver oxygen-rich blood to vital organs.

Chest compressions alone are very beneficial to a patient who is unresponsive and not breathing normally.

What is the difference between Clinical Death and Biological Death?

Clinical death occurs when a patient's heart stops beating and the blood stops circulating, cutting off oxygen and nourishment to the entire body. Since normal breathing rarely continues when the heart stops, clinical death means a patient has no respirations.

The reversal of clinical death is sometimes possible through immediate CPR, early defibrillation, and the quick deployment of other advanced life support treatments provided by Emergency Medical Services (EMS) or a hospital. Resuscitation after more than 4 to 6 minutes of clinical death is difficult, and if successful, can leave a patient with brain damage or brain death. However, longer intervals of clinical death have been survived by patients that are hypothermic (body core temperatures less than 35°C/95°F).

After 8 to 10 minutes of arrested circulation, tissue and brain damage may be so extensive that resuscitation is no longer possible. This is called *biological death*. Time is a critical factor between clinical and biological death. For each minute that passes without the necessary treatment the chances of survival fade dramatically.

Unresponsive Patients who are not Breathing Normally

Unresponsive patients who are not breathing normally may be in cardiac arrest. Rapid recognition of cardiac arrest is very important. After you've determined that a patient is unresponsive and not breathing normally, activate EMS immediately. Next, you begin CPR – chest compressions.

What does *unresponsive* mean? A patient who is unresponsive shows no sign of movement and does not respond in any way to stimulation, such as a tap on the collarbone or loud talking.

What does *not breathing normally* mean? An unresponsive adult, child or infant taking gasping breaths is NOT breathing normally. In the first few minutes after cardiac arrest, a patient may be barely breathing, or taking infrequent, slow and noisy gasps. Do not confuse this with normal breathing. An unresponsive patient barely breathing, or taking infrequent, slow and noisy gasps needs CPR immediately.

How do you determine if a patient is unresponsive and not breathing normally? First, check a child or adult patient's responsiveness level by delivering the Responder Statement and tapping the patient's collarbone to get a reaction. The Responder Statement is *"Hello? My name is _____. I'm an Emergency Responder. May I help you?"* Then, while tapping the patient, you ask *"Are you okay?"* Talking and tapping the patient allows you to survey the patient's responsiveness. To check the responsiveness of an infant you tap or pinch them and shout their name. You will learn how and when to deliver a Responder Statement and check for responsiveness during the Skill Development sessions.

A patient who is unresponsive shows no sign of movement and does not respond to stimulation, such as a tap on the collarbone or loud talking.

To check for breathing, you quickly *look* to see if the patient's chest is rising with each breath. Also, *listen* for breathing and *feel* expired air on your very sensitive ear. Obviously, if you don't see the chest rising, hear the air coming from his mouth or feel air on your ear then the patient is not breathing and needs emergency care immediately. You will learn how and when to perform this check for breathing during the Skill Development sessions.

NOTE – Emergency Responders do not take time to check for a pulse. Studies show that even healthcare providers have difficulty detecting a pulse on unresponsive patients. Checking for a pulse takes too much time. Instead, begin CPR immediately.

To check for breathing, you quickly *look* to see if the patient's chest is rising with each breath. Also, *listen* for breathing and *feel* expired air on your very sensitive ear. Remember, slow and noisy *gasps* from the patient is not normal breathing and typical within the first few minutes of sudden cardiac arrest.

Reasons for a Person to Stop Breathing

A person may not be breathing for a number of reasons. Here are ten:

1. Heart attack or sudden cardiac arrest
2. Submersion and near drowning
3. Stroke
4. Foreign body airway obstruction – choking
5. Smoke inhalation
6. Drug overdose
7. Electrocution, suffocation
8. Injuries
9. Lightning strike
10. Coma

How Rescue Breathing Works

If after providing chest compressions to an unresponsive patient you decide to give him rescue breaths, there is plenty of unused oxygen in your expired breath to help a nonbreathing patient. The air we breathe contains 21 percent oxygen. We use about five percent for ourselves. This leaves a very high percentage of oxygen in the air we exhale after each breath. The unused oxygen can be used for rescue breathing to support a nonbreathing patient. You will learn how to perform and will practice giving rescue breaths during your Skill Development and Scenario Practice session.

NOTE – If you are unable or feel uncomfortable giving an unresponsive patient rescue breaths – RELAX. Simply give the patient continuous chest compressions. Chest compressions alone are beneficial to a patient without a heartbeat. Your efforts will still help circulate blood that contains some oxygen.

There is plenty of unused oxygen in your expired breath to help a nonbreathing patient.

The Chain of Survival and You –
The Emergency Responder

The Chain of Survival illustrates the four links of patient care. It emphasizes the teamwork needed in emergency situations between you and professional emergency care providers. When you recognize a potentially life-threatening emergency, you help with the first three links in the Chain of Survival. The fourth link involves professional emergency care providers only – EMTs, Paramedics, nurses and doctors. Let's look at each of the four links in the Chain of Survival.

Study Questions

♦ What are the Chain of Survival's four links and which three involve an Emergency Responder?

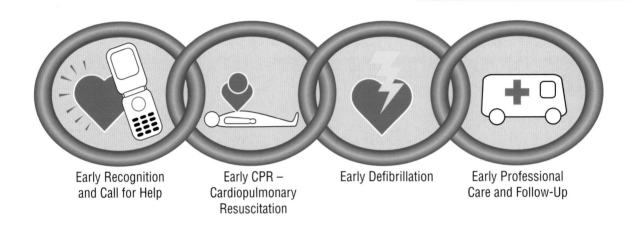

Early Recognition and Call for Help   Early CPR – Cardiopulmonary Resuscitation   Early Defibrillation   Early Professional Care and Follow-Up

Early Recognition and Call for Help

As an Emergency Responder, you must first recognize that an emergency exists. Once you've determined that an emergency exists, evaluate the scene to determine if it is safe for you to assist the patient. If it is safe for you to assist the patient, you next determine if the patient is responsive and breathing normally. If he is unresponsive and not breathing normally, you must rapidly activate the EMS in your local area. This link involves you the Emergency Responder.

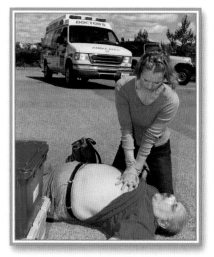

Early CPR – Cardiopulmonary Resuscitation

A person who is unresponsive and not breathing normally needs CPR immediately. Early CPR is the best treatment for cardiac arrests until a defibrillator and more advanced trained professionals arrive. Effective and immediate chest compressions prolong the window of time during which defibrillation can effectively occur and provide a small amount of blood flow to the heart, brain, and other vital organs. Immediate CPR can double or triple a patient's chance of survival when experiencing a sudden cardiac arrest. This link also involves you, the Emergency Responder.

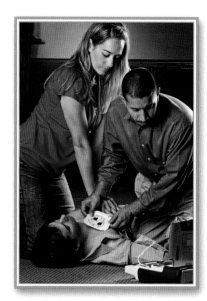

Early Defibrillation

Combined with CPR, early defibrillation by you, the Emergency Responder, or EMS personnel, significantly increases the probability of survival of a patient who suffers a sudden cardiac arrest. During this course you may learn how to use an Automated External Defibrillator (AED). If you witness a cardiac arrest and an AED is available, you should begin chest compressions and use the AED as soon as possible (more on this later). When applied to a person in cardiac arrest, an AED automatically analyzes the patient's heart rhythm and indicates if an electric shock is needed to help restore a normal heartbeat. By learning how to use an AED in this course, this link in the Chain of Survival involves you the Emergency Responder.

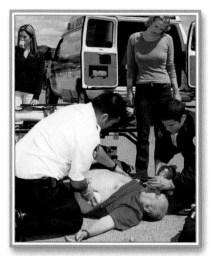

Early Professional Care and Follow-Up

EMS personnel and hospital staff can provide advanced patient care that you cannot. The advanced care EMS personnel and hospital staff can provide includes artificial airways, oxygen, cardiac drugs and surgical interventions. After initial on-scene care, EMS personnel take the patient to the hospital for more advanced medical procedures. The patient remains hospitalized until no longer needing constant, direct medical attention.

Using AB-CABS and the *Cycle of Care* to **Prioritize Emergency Care**

Remembering How To Help

If you are ever in a situation where you can help another in need, nervousness will be natural. Your nervousness can make it difficult to remember what to do and how to do it. To help you remember what to do, the memory word (mnemonic) AB-CABS can be used to remind you of the pathway and priorities of emergency care. By learning this memory word, you'll know what to do first, second, third and so on when a person with a life-threatening illness or injury needs you. The meaning and prioritized flow of AB-CABS is:

A = **A**ssess the scene for danger.
    Is the patient's **A**irway Open?

B = Is the patient **B**reathing Normally?

C = **C**hest **C**ompressions

A = **A**irway Open

B = **B**reathing for the Patient

S = **S**erious Bleeding, **S**hock, **S**pinal Injury

Study Questions

- What does the AB-CABS memory word mean?
- What is meant by the *Cycle of Care*?
- What do you do if you discover a patient is not breathing normally?
- What does "*Continually move through the Cycle of Care*" mean?

Cycle of Care: AB-CABS™

Continue Until Help or AED Arrives

A B
Airway Breathing
Open? Normally?

C
Chest
Compressions

A Airway Open

B **B**reathing
for Patient

S **S**erious Bleeding
Shock
Spinal Injury

In Australia and New Zealand, use the following ANZCOR Basic Life Support Flowchart (Guideline 8):

DRS ABCD

D = **D**angers?	Check for danger (hazards/risks/safety)
R = **R**esponsive?	Check for response (if unresponsive)
S = **S**end	Send for help
A = **A**irway	Open the airway
B = **B**reathing?	Check breathing (if not breathing /abnormal breathing)
C = **C**PR	Start CPR
D = **D**efibrillator	Attach an Automated External Defibrillator (AED) as soon as available and follow the prompts

Serious Bleeding, Shock and Spinal Injury

The "S" portion of the memory word AB-CAB**S** reminds Emergency Responders to manage **S**erious Bleeding, **S**hock and **S**pinal Injury. You can learn how to manage these three life-threatening emergencies in the Emergency First Response Primary Care (CPR) Course.

The AB-CABS *Cycle of Care* Graphic

When you first begin to assist a patient with a life-threatening illness or injury, reflect on a visual representation of the memory word AB-CABS. We call this visual representation the *Cycle of Care*. The *Cycle of Care* provides you with the correct pathway and priorities for emergency care. You continue using the *Cycle of Care* for a patient who is injured or ill until Emergency Medical Service personnel arrive and take over.

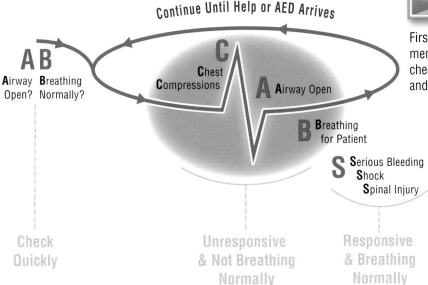

Cycle of Care: AB-CABS™

First begin with the "AB" portion of the memory word. This reminds you to quickly check to see if the patient's **A**irway is open and to note if he's **B**reathing normally.

Reading from left to right on the graphic you first begin with the <u>AB</u> portion of the memory word. This reminds you to quickly <u>A</u>ssess the scene for danger, check to see if the patient's <u>A</u>irway is open and to note if he's <u>B</u>reathing normally.

If a patient's airway is open but he's unresponsive and not breathing normally, move to the <u>CAB</u> portion of the memory word (in the blue sphere). The <u>CAB</u> portion of the memory word reminds you how to perform CPR. <u>CAB</u> means <u>C</u>hest <u>C</u>ompressions, open the <u>A</u>irway and then <u>B</u>reathe for the patient. If a patient is unresponsive and not breathing normally you must act immediately to provide <u>C</u>hest <u>C</u>ompressions. After <u>C</u>hest <u>C</u>ompressions you open the patient's <u>A</u>irway and then <u>B</u>reathe for the patient by giving rescue breaths.

Once you are finished providing rescue breaths for the patient, you return to <u>C</u>hest <u>C</u>ompressions and begin again. You continue CPR in a continuous cycle of chest compressions, re-opening the airway and providing rescue breaths. We call this the *Cycle of Care*.

If you find a patient who is responsive and breathing normally, then he does not need CPR. You SKIP all the steps in the blue sphere – the <u>CAB</u> portion of the memory word. In this situation you move along the *Cycle of Care* to the <u>S</u> portion of <u>CABS</u> and treat the patient for <u>S</u>erious bleeding, <u>S</u>hock and <u>S</u>pinal injury. Notice that if you are performing CPR on a patient who is not breathing normally you continue with <u>C</u>hest <u>C</u>ompressions, opening the <u>A</u>irway and providing rescue <u>B</u>reaths – <u>CAB</u>. CPR takes priority over most other concerns.

Continually Move Through the *Cycle Of Care*

Regardless of a patient's situation upon your arrival, you begin a primary assessment using the memory word AB-CABS to help you remember how to begin and what steps to follow. Remember the word AB-CABS and think of the *Cycle of Care* graphic.

The phrase, "*Continually move through the Cycle of Care*" helps you maintain appropriate emergency care sequencing. In a continual *Cycle of Care* you deliver CPR, remembering the **CAB** portion of the memory word. You do this until professional help (ambulance or EMS) arrives or an Automated External Defibrillator (AED) is located and brought to the patient. More detail on AEDs will follow later.

Cycle of Care: AB-CABS™

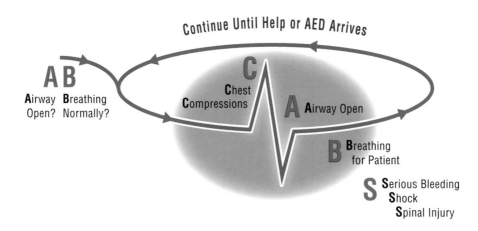

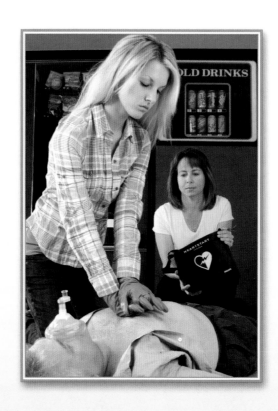

Helping Others in Need

If you encounter someone who needs emergency care and you've assessed the scene for your own personal safety, you should render assistance immediately – even seconds count. The chances of successful resuscitation diminish rapidly with time. When a person has no heartbeat and is not breathing normally, irreversible brain damage can occur within minutes. Many medical emergencies, such as sudden cardiac arrest, require the secondary assistance of EMS personnel and hospital care. Get EMS on the scene fast – seconds count. It is typically best to alert the EMS first, before rendering emergency care (more on this later). Besides providing an act of kindness toward a fellow human being in need, there are three basic reasons for assisting someone who needs emergency care:

Study Questions

- Why is time critical when someone needs emergency care?
- Why should you assist someone who needs emergency care?
- What are six reasons people hesitate to provide emergency care to a patient – even if they are CPR trained?

1. You can save or restore a patient's life.

2. You can help reduce a patient's recovery time; either in the hospital or at home.

3. You can make the difference between a patient having a temporary or lifelong disability.

Some individuals, even when CPR and first aid trained, hesitate to provide emergency care to those in need. This is understandable and there are legitimate concerns on the part of Emergency Responders when helping those with injuries and illnesses. The six most common reasons why people hesitate to provide emergency care are:

1. **Anxiety.**

    People may hesitate due to general nervousness or anxiousness. This is a perfectly normal reaction when helping those in need. However, as it's been emphasized, trust your training. When you follow the priorities of care as outlined in this course, you are giving your patient the best chance for survival or revival.

2. **Guilt.**

    People may hesitate when thinking about how they might feel if the patient doesn't recover after delivering first aid. You can't guarantee that a patient will live or fully recover – there's too much beyond anyone's control. Be confident that any help you offer is a contribution to another human being and has the potential to make a difference in the patient's outcome. Even in the worst of outcomes, you can take comfort in the fact that you used your skills and gave the patient more of a chance than he had alone.

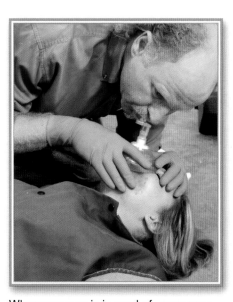

When someone is in need of emergency care, you should render assistance immediately – even seconds count.

3. **Fear of imperfect performance.**

    People may hesitate because they feel they cannot properly help an injured or ill person. It is seldom true that the smallest error will hurt or kill a patient. During this course, you will learn what's critical and what's not. If you focus on perfection, you'll have a tendency to do nothing in a real emergency. Don't get caught in that trap – it's not hard to provide adequate care, and *adequate care provided is always better than perfect care withheld.*

4. **Fear of making a person worse.**

The most serious medical emergency is when a patient isn't breathing normally and has no heartbeat. Sometimes people hesitate to help such a patient, fearing they will make him worse. As an Emergency Responder, realize that you cannot make such a person worse. A person with no breathing and no heartbeat is already in the worst state of health. You can trust your training. Take a moment to relax, think of your training, then step forward and help.

5. **Fear of infection.**

People may hesitate because they are afraid of being infected by the person they are assisting. Keep in mind that a large percentage of all CPR is performed in the home or for a loved one or friend. In these cases, risk of infection is low and fear of infection should not cause you to withhold CPR or emergency care. Infection is a concern, but your training includes learning to use protective barriers to minimize the risk of disease transmission. By using barriers, you're highly unlikely to get any disease or infection from someone you help. Further, research has shown that the chance of disease transmission is very rare when providing CPR.

6. **Responsibility concerns.**

People may hesitate because they are afraid of being sued. In general, the fear of being sued should not stop Emergency Responders from providing emergency care. In many regions of the world, Good Samaritan laws (or regional equivalents) have been put in place to encourage people to come to the aid of others.

Good Samaritan Laws

Good Samaritan laws (or regional equivalents) are enacted to encourage people to come to the aid of others. In general, they protect individuals who voluntarily offer assistance to those in need. They are created to provide immunity against liability.

Often, a Good Samaritan law imposes no legal duty to help a stranger in need. However, local laws may vary on this point and in some areas people are required to provide aid. There may not be Good Samaritan laws in your local area. It would be wise to determine the extent and use of local Good Samaritan laws. Your Emergency First Response Instructor may be able to provide you with information about Good Samaritan laws in your local region. In general, there are six ways you should act to be protected by Good Samaritan laws. They are:

1. Only provide care that is within the scope of your training as an Emergency Responder.

2. Ask for permission to help

3. Act in good faith.

4. Do not be reckless or negligent.

5. Act as a prudent person would.

6. Do not abandon the patient once you begin care. The exception to this is if you must do so to protect yourself from imminent danger.

Study Questions

- What is a Good Samaritan law?
- In general, what are the six ways you should act to be protected by most Good Samaritan laws?

Good Samaritan laws are enacted to encourage people to come to the aid of others.

The Emotional Aspects of Being an **Emergency Responder**

Helping another person in need is satisfying and feels good. Depending on the circumstances, however, it may also produce a certain amount of stress and some fearfulness. In many cases, a little stress may actually assist you when helping others by preparing you physically and mentally.

CPR is No Guarantee of a Successful Outcome

As discussed earlier, CPR is a two-step process – pressing on a patient's chest and breathing for the person. CPR is a temporary measure that can extend the window of opportunity for the patient to be revived. CPR, the use of an AED, and some types of first aid are inherently emotional activities. However, as an Emergency Responder you should never fear harming a patient, especially when performing CPR on an individual who is unresponsive and not breathing normally. Why? Simply put, you really cannot make the person worse. A person that is unresponsive and not breathing normally is already in the worse state of health possible since he probably does not have a heartbeat. If you perform CPR as outlined in this course, you really cannot make the patient worse than when you first found the individual. You don't need to fear providing CPR. Perform CPR to the best of your ability. Trust your training. If your efforts to revive a person in need do not succeed, focus on the fact that you tried your best to help.

But, if you could have provided CPR and where available, used an AED and didn't, you may spend the rest of your life wondering if it could have made a difference. Don't let that happen, again, trust your training. Adequate care provided is better than perfect care withheld.

CPR and some types of first aid are inherently emotional activities. However, as an Emergency Responder you should never fear harming a patient when performing CPR on someone who is unresponsive and not breathing normally.

Study Questions

- Why should you never fear harming a patient when performing CPR on an unresponsive patient who is not breathing normally?

- How can you care for yourself as an Emergency Responder after you've provided emergency care in stressful situations?

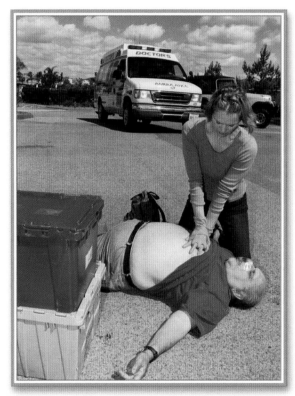

CPR, the use of an AED, and some types of first aid are inherently emotional activities. However, as an Emergency Responder you should never fear harming a patient, especially when performing CPR on an individual who is unresponsive and not breathing normally.

You may have elevated physical and emotional stress after providing emergency care. If you do, try the following:

▶ Try to relax after the incident. Lower your heartbeat and blood pressure by resting or walking slowly. Relaxing will reduce elevated adrenaline produced by your body to help you through the stress of providing emergency care.

▶ Avoid stimuli such as caffeine, nicotine or alcohol.

▶ Talk about the incident to others. Sharing your experience with others helps in processing thoughts and emotions, therefore reducing stress and anxiety. Talk can be a healing medicine.

▶ If you experience physical or emotional problems such as prolonged depression, sleeping disorders, persistent anxiety or eating disorders, seek the help of a health care professional.

▶ Spend time with others. Reach out – people care.

Responders In Action

As an Emergency Responder, if you provide care for an injured or ill person, we'd like to hear about it. Incidents need not be dramatic or involve a life-threatening condition. Sharing these stories not only encourages others to use their skills, but also helps monitor and gauge the effectiveness of Emergency First Response training and assists in future course development. Submit story online by going to www.emergencyfirstresponse.com.

Recognizing Life-Threatening Emergencies

When you witness a serious car accident or watch someone take a bad fall, it's reasonable to assume the patient will have life-threatening injuries. Even if you don't see it occur, many accident scenes clearly point to medical emergencies. Unfortunately, not all life-threatening emergencies are so obvious. Some serious conditions occur due to illness or subtle accidents. Sometimes the patient's symptoms come on quickly and other times the patient gets progressively worse over time. Because time is critical, as you've already learned, you need to be able to recognize all life-threatening conditions and then provide appropriate emergency medical care.

Heart Attack

A *heart attack* occurs when blood flow to part of the patient's heart is stopped or greatly reduced. Heart attack patients commonly complain of *stabbing* chest pain behind the breastbone and an uncomfortable pressure or squeezing - often described as a tight band around their chest. This usually lasts for more than a few minutes, or goes away and comes back. The pain is sometimes described as an ache, or feeling similar to heartburn or indigestion. Pain or other sensations such as tingling (pins and needles), numbness or heaviness can be experienced in the patient's arms (frequently the left arm) or jaw. Patients may also complain of nausea, rapid heartbeat, shortness of breath and dizziness or lightheadedness. They may frequently sweat profusely are noticeably pale and may feel faint.

Often, heart attack patients deny that anything is seriously wrong. This is especially true when symptoms are mild or go away temporarily. If you suspect a heart attack, do not delay in calling EMS. The longer the heart goes without adequate blood flow, the more permanent damage is likely to occur.

Cardiac Arrest

Cardiac arrest is when normal circulation of the blood through the heart and body stops due to a failure of the heart to beat effectively. Cardiac arrest is different from a heart attack, but cardiac arrest may be caused by the same reduced blood flow to the heart muscle that causes a heart attack.

Normal circulation of the blood through the heart and body stops when the heart begins to beat too fast (*ventricular tachycardia*), quiver erratically (*ventricular fibrillation*), or just stop beating. Although cardiac arrest is most often caused by heart disease or heart defects, it can occur any time regular heart rhythms are disturbed. Sudden cardiac arrest may occur independently from a heart attack and often is without any discernible warning signs.

Study Questions

- What causes heart attacks and cardiac arrest.
- How can you recognize if a patient is having a heart attack or is in cardiac arrest?
- How can you recognize heart related emergencies in children?
- What is the universal sign for "choking?"

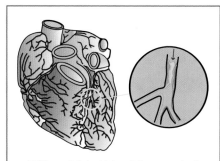

With restricted blood flow, part of the heart muscle begins to die.

Heart attack patients commonly complain of chest pain and an uncomfortable pressure or squeezing.

Besides a patient suddenly collapsing, there are two ways to recognize cardiac arrest. First, the patient does not respond when you speak to or touch him. He is unresponsive and not moving. Second, the patient does not appear to have any signs of life and – he is not breathing normally. Beginning CPR quickly and providing defibrillation as quickly as possible are critical to patient survival.

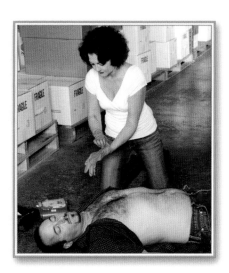

Heart Problems in Children and Infants

Infants and children rarely suffer cardiac arrest because, with very few exceptions, they have healthy hearts. However, as a result of stopping breathing, infants and children do go on to suffer cardiac arrest if their breathing is not supported or restored. In the same way as with adults, assess whether the collapsed child is unresponsive and not breathing normally. If they are unresponsive and not breathing normally, deliver CPR. The major difference is that with infants and children defibrillation is rarely required.

Complete (Severe) Airway Obstruction

Complete airway obstruction usually results when a patient chokes on food, although any object placed in the mouth could end up blocking the patient's airway. Recognizing airway obstruction is important because the patient can't breathe. Patients also tend to become embarrassed and try to leave the area.

You may suspect choking if a patient grasps or clutches the neck or throat area. This is the universal distress signal for choking. By asking the patient what's wrong, you can determine if the patient can speak, is breathing or is able to cough. A patient with a complete or severe airway obstruction may become unconscious if the airway is not cleared quickly.

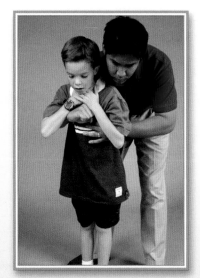

Asking a Patient for **Permission to Help**

When an injured or ill responsive adult or child needs emergency care, ask permission before you assist them. Asking for permission to help reassures the patient, by indicating that you are trained appropriately. You ask for permission to help with the Responder Statement. You simply say, *Hello? My name is _____. I'm an Emergency Responder. May I help you?*

It's important to get the patient's agreement if he is alert and responsive. If the patient agrees or doesn't respond, you can proceed with emergency care. There is implied permission – meaning you can proceed with emergency care – if the patient is unresponsive. If an injured or ill responsive adult refuses emergency care, do not force it on the person. If possible, talk with the individual and monitor the patient's condition by observation without providing actual care. You could, however, activate EMS at this time.

Study Question

◆ How do you ask for permission to help a patient?

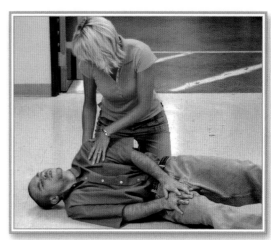

When an injured or ill responsive adult needs emergency care, ask permission before you assist the person. Asking for permission to help reassures the patient, noting that you are trained appropriately.

Hello? My name is

_____

I'm an Emergency Responder. May I help you?

Activating the Emergency Medical Service – *Call First* and *Care First*

In the Chain of Survival your role as the Emergency Responder is to summon emergency medical aid and to assist the patient until it arrives. Activating EMS is so important that in most circumstances, if you're alone and there's no one else to activate the EMS for you, you *Call First*, then assist the patient.

After establishing patient unresponsiveness, and identifying that he is not breathing normally, ask a bystander to call EMS and secure an AED if possible. If you are alone, use your mobile phone to call EMS. If you do not have a mobile phone, leave the patient to call EMS if no other option exists. This is the *Call First* approach to emergency care. You *Call First* to activate EMS, then you provide assistance.

There are two primary exceptions to the *Call First* approach to emergency care. In the following instances, you provide *Care First*, then call EMS:

Study Questions

◆ When should you activate the Emergency Medical Services (EMS) once you find an unresponsive adult or child who needs emergency care?

◆ What are two exceptions to the *Call First* approach to emergency care. How do you provide *Care First* in your particular region?

◆ How do you activate Emergency Medical Services (EMS) in your area?

1. If the patient is a child or an adult who has experienced submersion in water. In these cases, you provide CPR for a short time, particularly rescue breaths to the patient, and then call EMS. This is called *Care First*.

   NOTE – Two regional resuscitation organizations define providing Care First for a *short time* differently. In North, South and Central America, Asia and the Pacific Island countries (AHA Guidelines), it's defined as providing care for approximately 2 minutes; the European Resuscitation Council (ERC) guidelines define a *short time* as 1 minute. In Australia and New Zealand (ARC/NZRC Guidelines) a short time isn't defined – provide Care First for 1-2 minutes, then call EMS.

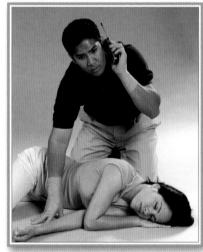

Call First means that if you're alone and there's no one else to activate the Emergency Medical Service for you, you *Call First,* then assist the patient.

2. With children and infants, if you are alone, you should provide CPR – *Care First* – then call EMS and retrieve an AED if close by. Provide this *Care First* based on your region:

▶ American Heart Association (AHA) Guidelines – Provide five sets of CPR, then call EMS.

▶ European Resuscitation Council (ERC) Guidelines – Provide five initial rescue breaths followed by approximately one minute of CPR, then call EMS.

With EMS on the way, the care you provide increases the chance that advanced care will help the patient when it arrives. Your training in this course is based on handling emergencies where you have an EMS system in place. If you need to provide emergency aid in areas away from EMS support, you should continue your education with more advanced first aid training.

In my local area, the Emergency Medical Service (EMS) is activated by calling:

Irregular Heart Rhythms **and** Using AEDs

A healthy heart will normally beat between 60 to 100 beats per minute. This heartbeat is triggered by regular, well-organized electrical impulses.

Sometimes heart damage or injury to the heart muscle can cause the heart rhythm to become erratic and fast. This irregular heart rhythm does not generate a life-giving pulse and the patient suffers a cardiac arrest.

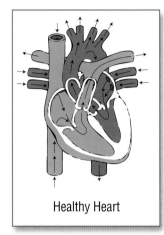

Healthy Heart

Study Questions

- What can cause a normal heart rhythm to become erratic and fast?
- What is *defibrillation* and why is it important to a patient whose heart has stopped?
- How can a patient's erratic heartbeat be restored to a normal heart rhythm?
- What is an Automated External Defibrillator (AED)?
- When is an AED used?
- What special considerations need to be taken when applying an AED to a person who is wearing a transdermal medication patch, a pacemaker or an implanted defibrillator?
- What special considerations need to be taken when applying an AED to a pregnant woman?
- What special precautions are necessary when using an AED on a patient laying on a wet surface?
- What should you do if you forget the steps for using an AED?
- Why and how often should an AED be inspected?

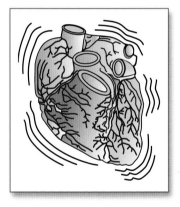

One such irregular heart rhythm is called *ventricular fibrillation* – a rhythm where the heart just quivers. This irregular heart rhythm does not generate a life-giving pulse and the patient suffers a cardiac arrest.

An irregular heart rhythm is potentially reversible with a *defibrillator*. You will use an Automated External Defibrillator or AED to deliver an electrical shock, disrupting the abnormal heart rhythms. The momentary disruption can allow the heart's normal heartbeat to return.

Administering an electrical shock from an AED is called *defibrillation*. Prompt and early defibrillation of a patient's abnormal heart rhythm is a vital part of the Chain of Survival.

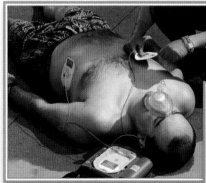

Prompt and early defibrillation of a patient's abnormal heart rhythm is a vital part of the Chain of Survival.

How AEDs Work

An AED is a computerized and portable electronic machine that automatically analyses the cause of the cardiac arrest and where appropriate, delivers a shock to a patient in cardiac arrest. In some cases cardiac arrest is not treated by a shock and the AED can reliably detect these rhythms and direct you to provide CPR until the EMS arrive.

AEDs are extremely reliable and if used inappropriately on a collapsed patient who does have a pulse, an AED will not shock. With treatable cardiac arrest the shock delivered by the AED tries to stop the heart's abnormal activity so as to allow it to reorganize into a pulse generating rhythm.

AEDs connect to a patient via two chest pads – each having an adhesive gel on one side of the pad to stick to the patient's chest. When the AED is turned on, its computer analyzes the patient's need for a shock. If the AED detects a shockable heart rhythm, the AED will indicate that a shock is advised. Depending on the type of AED, you will either activate the shock by pressing a button or the machine administers the shock automatically. You will learn how to use a specific AED model during the skills portion of this course.

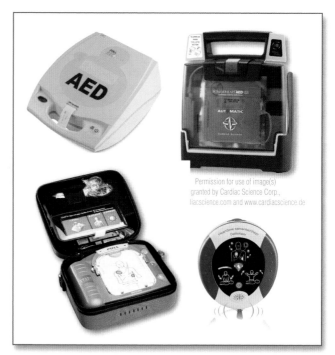

Permission for use of image(s) granted by Cardiac Science Corp., liacscience.com and www.cardiacscience.de

An AED is a computerized and portable electronic machine that automatically analyses the cause of the cardiac arrest and where appropriate, delivers a shock to a patient in cardiac arrest.

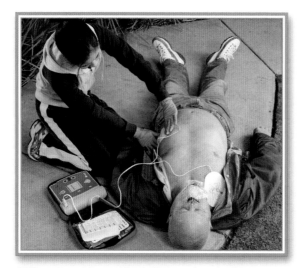

AEDs connect to a patient via two chest pads

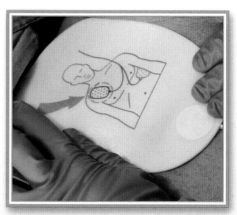

Manual Vs. Automated Defibrillators

If you've watched hospital docudramas on television, no doubt you've seen nurses and doctors use a *manual* defibrillator on a patient whose heart has a shockable, abnormal heart rhythm. These manual defibrillators are very different from the sophisticated, yet simple to operate AEDs you'll use as a lay Emergency Responder.

Manual Defibrillator   Automated Defibrillator

In a hospital setting, patients are connected to a device telling doctors how a patient's heart is behaving. If the patient's heart begins an abnormal rhythm they know immediately. To activate the *manual* defibrillator they must first turn it on, set it at a specific energy level for electrical discharge, retrieve two paddles from the unit, apply conducting gel to each and strategically place the paddles on the patient's chest. Once on the chest, doctors can provide a shock to the patient often by pressing buttons on the paddles. Hospital-based manual defibrillators vary in usage, but the equipment and technique described here is common.

An AED on the other hand does all the work for you when you need to assist a patient whose heart is in ventricular tachycardia or fibrillation. This why the word "automated" is part of this device's name. Often, you won't even need to turn it on. With some units, just lifting the device's lid or removing the adhesive pads from the unit turns it on. When using an AED you won't need a separate heart-monitoring device as in a hospital, because the AED automatically analyzes the patient's heart rhythm once the pads are in place. Also in contrast to a manual defibrillator, you won't need to set the AED at a specific energy level or apply conducting gel. AEDs are simple and easy to use.

Using an AED

To treat sudden cardiac arrest, lay rescuers must be able to rapidly integrate CPR with AED use. To give the patient the best chance of survival, three actions must occur within the first moments of a cardiac arrest.

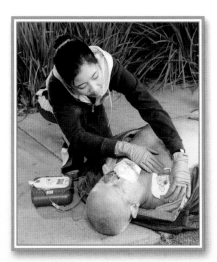

1. **Alert the Emergency Medical Service.** Call EMS or if you are at work, activate your specific emergency medical response procedure.

2. **Use the AED on a patient as quickly as possible.** The faster you defibrillate a shockable heart rhythm, the better the chances a patient has of a full recovery. Because AEDs are automatic, they're not difficult to use. Follow all manufacturer instructions. AEDs give verbal instructions to the user as well as visual instructions for the hearing impaired. More on this topic will follow during the skills portion of the course.

3. **Provide CPR when told by the AED to do so.** CPR combined with the use of an AED increases the patient's chances of survival.

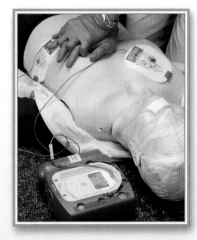

When to Use an AED

With these three actions in mind, let's outline the *ideal* sequence you would use, should you confirm that an adult or child patient is unresponsive and not breathing normally, *and* you know where an AED is located:

1. **If You are Alone**

   ▶ **Call EMS.** Use your mobile phone to call EMS. If you do not have a mobile phone, leave the patient to call EMS if no other option exists. Consider yelling for help to attract bystanders.

   ▶ **Retrieve the AED.** After alerting EMS, retrieve an AED if know one is close by.

   ▶ **Set up and use the AED.** If the AED indicates a shock, deliver the shock (some AEDs automatically deliver the shock).

   ▶ **Begin CPR.** After the shock is delivered, immediately begin CPR. If no shock is indicated by the AED, immediately begin CPR and continue as directed by the machine's prompts.

2. **If Bystander's Are Available**

   ▶ **Immediately Begin CPR.** While giving CPR you can direct bystanders to assist you. The immediate delivery of chest compressions with minimal interruptions is very important.

   ▶ **Alert EMS.** While giving the patient CPR, send a bystander to call EMS.

   ▶ **Retrieve the AED.** While giving the patient CPR, send a bystander to retrieve an AED – it can be the same bystander that calls EMS.

   ▶ **Set up and use the AED.** Once the AED arrives, continue CPR if at all possible. If the bystander is trained or able to follow your instructions they may be able to set up the AED for use while you continue CPR. If this is not possible, you must stop CPR and promptly set up the AED for use. If the AED indicates a shock is needed, deliver the shock (some AEDs automatically deliver the shock). After the shock is delivered, immediately begin CPR again, (some AEDs provide step by step CPR instructions). If no shock is indicated by the AED, continue giving CPR as directed by the machine's prompts.

Special AED Considerations

When using AEDs there are a few special considerations to keep in mind.

Children – The incidence of cardiac arrest in children is low compared to adults. Causes of cardiac arrest in children are: 1) airway and breathing problems, 2) traumatic injuries and accidents, and 3) heart disease from rare birth defects. Occasionally children will require defibrillation with an AED. Adult AEDs are suitable for use on children older than 8 years. For children between 1 and 8 years old, special child-sized pads may be available. However, if a child-specific method of delivering a reduced shock to a child is not available, use adult pads and shock doses. Never use child pads on an adult.

Infants – There are case reports demonstrating successful use of AEDs on infants. However, AED use on infants is not supported by definitive research. For this reason AED use by lay Emergency Responders on infants is not recommended.

Chest Hair – AED pad to skin contact is very important for successful defibrillation. If a patient's chest is extremely hairy, consider shaving the area where the AED pads are placed. Some AEDs may include small shavers in their container. Regardless, avoid unnecessary delays to pad placement and AED use. Seconds count.

Wet Chest and Surface – If a patient's chest is wet or sweaty, dry it before applying the AED pads. This will allow for better pad adhesion and delivery of the shock to the patient. Some AEDs will prompt for better pad adhesion if they are not sticking to the patient properly. Again, avoid unnecessary delays to pad placement and AED use. Seconds count. You can defibrillate on a wet surface as long as all safety rules are observed and manufacturer's instructions followed. There are no reports of harm to rescuers from attempting defibrillation in wet environments. Your instructor will guide you relative to the specific AED you'll use in the course.

Metal Surface – You can defibrillate on a metal surface as long as all safety rules are observed and manufacturer instructions followed. Electricity always takes the path of least resistance and this is between the two pads through the patients chest - not through a metal surface. Your instructor will guide you relative to the specific AED you'll use in the course.

Medicated Skin Patches and Dressings – Never place AED pads directly on top of a medicated skin patch. An entire AED pad must be in direct contact with the patient's skin. Therefore, remove all bandages, dressings and medicated skin patches that impedes the pad's direct contact with the patient.

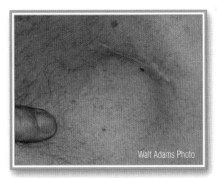

Implanted Defibrillator

Implanted Pacemakers and Defibrillators – Some patients may have implanted pacemakers and/or defibrillators. You can detect these devices when the patient's chest is exposed. Typically you'll see a small rectangular bump located just under the skin in the upper chest on the left side – about the size of a playing card. If the patient simply has a pacemaker, go ahead and use the AED as directed by the device. If a patient has an implanted defibrillator, an AED is not needed unless the device is not working. You'll hear the device deliver shocks and see the patient's muscles contracting if the device is working.

Pregnant Women – There is no evidence that shocks from an AED have adverse effects on the mother or baby. You should use an AED on a pregnant woman exactly the same as any other adult patient.

Emergency Responder Safety – Do not touch the patient while defibrillating. Touching a patient while a shock is being delivered could shock you. Also, do not use an AED when around flammable or combustible materials such as gasoline. Even though free-flowing oxygen can be flammable, there are no reports of fires caused by sparking when shocks were delivered.

AED Analysis – Do not touch the patient while the AED is analyzing his heart rhythm. Touching the patient may interfere with the analysis. Interestingly, mobile phones and radios will not interfere with AED analysis.

AED Maintenance

An AED may reverse clinical death when applied quickly and if the device is functioning properly. However, research indicates that failure to properly maintain defibrillators or power supplies is responsible for the majority of reported malfunctions.

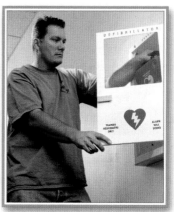

Most AED machines will perform a self-test, but you should turn the device on regularly to ensure it is operating properly.

In addition to regular preventative maintenance, AED manufacturers recommend daily inspection. There are two reasons for daily inspection of an AED. First, it ensures it will always be ready for your use in an emergency and second, to make sure you stay familiar with the unit's operation. You should check to make sure all of the proper supplies are available, that the device is operational and not damaged in any way, and that the batteries are in working order. AEDs have indicator lights/symbols to conform their status and under no circumstances should AEDs be turned on to check they are working – this will drain the battery unnecessarily. Also, check replacement dates for items such as batteries and electrode pads. Further, most AEDs perform a silent series of self-tests and should a fault be identified a visual and/or audible warning will be given.

Why Do AED Pads Expire?

AED pads expire for a number of reasons and they all deal with hampering the pads ability to stick to and provide proper connectivity with a patient. AED pads must make good skin contact with the patient. Good skin contact allows the AED to:

▶ Correctly analyze the patient's heart rhythm, determining if the patient requires a shock or not.

▶ Effectively deliver a lifesaving shock.

Assisting AED pads to adhere to the skin properly is a gel applied to the pads when they are manufactured. This gel actually enters into the pores of the patient's skin, acting as a conductivity bond between the patient and the pads. Over time, this gel dries out and breaks down chemically. AED pads used beyond their expiration date may not adhere well to the patient. During the rigors of CPR they may further lose their adhesion and thus their ability to analyze or deliver a lifesaving shock. Further, the electrical wires connected to the pads may begin to corrode.

With a few exceptions, AEDs do not test the condition of the pad even where they are pre-connected to the device. For this reason, manufacturers print expiration dates on their AED pads. The typical life expectancy of AED pads is between one to two years from the date of manufacture – sometimes more. Keep fresh AED pads with an AED. If the gel is dry on a set of pads, do not use them. Switch to fresh pads.

Your workplace may have an "AED Coordinator" whose job it is to conduct daily AED checks to make sure the corporate AEDs are regularly maintained and functioning properly. It's likely that this individual uses an AED maintenance and supply checklist designed to identify and prevent device deficiencies. A sample, generic checklist is provided. If the manufacturer of an AED and/or a regional government body provides specific checklists, use them instead.

Anyone tasked to oversee AED checks and maintenance should complete all required paperwork properly as per the AED manufacturer recommendations, company protocols and regional government regulations. In the unlikely event of an AED failing during an emergency, these documents will be important. Should an AED fail in use simply focus on CPR until the EMS arrive with their equipment.

Emergency First Response®
Automated External Defibrillator
Maintenance and Supply Checklist*

*Use one checklist per AED.

Inspection by_____ Date _____

AED Serial Number_____ Location in Building _____

Location – Accessibility

☐ Accessible and Visible?

☐ Cabinet Intact?

☐ Cabinet Alarm Operable? Alarm in "On" Position?

AED Inspection

☐ AED Damage? Dirt? Contamination?

☐ AED Case in Tact?

☐ Battery Installed?

☐ Status Light/Indicator?

☐ Service Light?

☐ Ready for Use?

AED Pads

☐ AED Pads in Case and in Sealed Packets?

☐ Pad Expiration Dates Current?

☐ Extra Pads?

☐ Adult and Child Pads?

Supplies

☐ Ventilation Barrier(s)?

☐ Exam Glove(s)?

☐ Razor(s)?

☐ Scissors?

☐ Small Towel or Paper Towels?

☐ Other items stored with AED: _____

_____

Comments and Corrective Actions Taken:

_____

_____

_____

_____

_____

CPR & AED Knowledge Review

Name: _____ Date: _____

1. Specific to emergency care, define the following groups by age:

   Adult_____*TEEN ↗*_____

   Child_____*1 → 12 Ø TEEN*_____

   Infant_____*1 4R ↓*_____

2. Primary Assessment: *(Check all that apply.)*

   ___✓___ a. Is always the first step of any emergency care.

   _____ b. Providing direct pressure on a bleeding wound.

   ___✓___ c. Is an Emergency Responder's first evaluation of an injured or ill person.

3. CPR stands for:___*CARDIO PULMINARY RECESSITATION*___

4. Chest compressions:

   _____ a. Always revive patients that are unresponsive and not breathing normally.

   _____ b. Should only be given by professional such as paramedics and doctors.

   ___✓___ c. Manually forces blood from the heart through the arteries and deliver oxygen-rich blood to vital organs.

5. CPR extends the window of opportunity for ___*RECESSITATION*___ – greatly increasing the patient's chance of revival.

6. You determine if a child or adult is unresponsive by:

   ___✓___ a. Delivering the Responder Statement and tapping the patient's collarbone.

   _____ b. Shaking the patient.

   _____ c. Listening for breathing.

7. List two reasons why a person may stop breathing.

   1.___*CHOKING*_____

   2.___*HEART ATTACK*_____

8. Name the Chain of Survival's four links in the spaces below.

   a.___*EARLY REC CALL FOR HELP*___ b.___*EARLY CPR*___ c.___*EARLY DEFIB*___ d.___*EARLY TRANSPORT PROF. CARE*___

9. Fill in the missing meaning for each letter on the *Cycle of Care* graphic.

   C = ___*CHEST COMPRESSIONS*___

   A = ___*AIRWAY*___

   B = ___*BREATHING*___

   S = ___*SERIOUS BLEEDING SHOCK SPINAL INJURY*___

Cycle of Care: AB-CABS™

Continue Until Help or AED Arrives

AB
Airway Breathing
Open? Normally?

C A B

10. The phrase, "*continually move through the Cycle of Care*" helps you maintain appropriate __EMERGENCY__ *1-9*
    __CARE SEQUENCING__.

11. When someone needs emergency care, time is critical because: *(Check all that apply.)*
    _____ a. It becomes more difficult to administer first aid.
    __✓__ b. The chances of successful resuscitation diminish with time.
    __✓__ c. When a person has no heartbeat and is not breathing, irreversible brain damage can occur within minutes.

12. Give three reasons why you should assist someone who needs emergency care: *1-10*
    a. _____ SAVE RESTORE LIFE
    b. _____ REDUCE RECOVERY TIME
    c. _____ ↓ LIFE LONG DISABILITY

13. Of the six reasons causing people to hesitate when providing emergency care to a patient, name three: *1-10/1-11*
    a. _____ ANXIETY
    b. _____ INFECTION
    c. _____ LAW SUIT

14. Good Samaritan laws are enacted to encourage people to come to the aid of others. Generally, they protect individuals who voluntarily offer assistance to those in need.   *1-11*
    __✓__ True _____ False

15. To be protected by Good Samaritan laws you should: *(Check all that apply.)*
    __✓__ a. Only provide care that is within the scope of your training as an Emergency Responder.
    __✓__ b. Ask for permission to help
    __✓__ c. Act in good faith.   *1-11*
    __✓__ d. Do not be reckless or negligent.
    _____ e. Avoid helping an injured or ill person when others are around.
    __✓__ f. Act as a prudent person would.
    __✓__ g. Do not abandon the patient once you begin care. The exception to this is if you must do so to protect yourself from imminent danger.

16. Why should you never fear harming a patient when performing CPR on an individual who is unresponsive and is not breathing normally?
    _____ YOU CAN'T MAKE IT WORSE   *1-12*
    _____
    _____

17. Providing emergency care can be stressful. How can you care for yourself after you've provided assistance in a stressful situation?
    _____ a. Spend time with others after providing care. Reach out for help.   *1-13*
    _____ b. Seek the help of a health care professional.
    _____ c. Talk about the incident to others.
    __✓__ d. All of the above.

18. Heart attack patients commonly complain of: *(Check all that apply.)*
    _____ a. severe leg pain
    __✓__ b. stabbing chest pain behind the breastbone   *1-14*
    __✓__ c. nausea, rapid heartbeat, shortness of breath and dizziness
    __✓__ d. pain or other sensations such as tingling, numbness or heaviness in the patient's arms or jaw

19. To ask a patient for permission to help, you deliver the Responder Statement. The complete statement is:
    _____ HI MY NAME IS – – – –
    _____ I'm AN EMERGENCY RESPONDER   *1-3*
    _____ MAY I HELP YOU?   *1-16*

20. Activating EMS is so important that in most circumstances (especially with adults), if you're alone and there's no one else to activate the EMS for you, you:

_____ a. Always give *Care First*. 1-17

___✓___ b. *Call First*, then assist the patient.

21. In your local area, the Emergency Medical Service (EMS) is activated by dialing:

_____911_____ (wk - 9-911)

22. Heart damage or injury to the heart can cause a normal heart rhythm to become erratic and fast. 1-18

___✓___ True _____ False

23. Defibrillation by an AED is the momentary disruption of an abnormal heart rhythm, allowing the heart's normal heartbeat to return.

___✓___ True _____ False 1-18

24. An AED connects to a patient via:

_____ a. Two wires implanted in the skin. 1-19

_____ b. A head band.

___✓___ c. Two pads with adhesive gel on the back.

25. AEDs give verbal and visual instructions making them easy to use.

___✓___ True _____ False

26. If a patient in cardiac arrest has a bandage or medicated skin patch located where an AED pad needs to be placed, you should:

___✓___ a. Remove the bandage or medicated patch and wipe the skin dry before placing the AED pad.

_____ b. Place the AED pad next to the medicated patch. 1-22

_____ c. Place the AED pad right over the medicated patch.

27. There is no evidence that shocks from an AED have adverse effects on the mother or baby. You should use an AED on a pregnant woman exactly the same as any other adult patient.

___✓___ True _____ False 1-22

28. CPR combined with the use of an AED increases the patient's chances of survival. 1.20

___✓___ True _____ False

29. Regarding AED defibrillation on a wet surface:

_____ a. This should never be done.

___✓___ b. You can defibrillate on a wet surface as long as all safety rules are observed and manufacturer's instructions followed. 1-22

_____ c. Use special AED pads in this circumstance.

30. In addition to regular preventative maintenance, AED manufacturers recommend ___DAILY___ inspection by those who are trained to use them.

_____ a. monthly 1-23

_____ b. weekly

___✓___ c. daily

Section TWO

Skills WORKBOOK

Contents

CPR & AED

CPR & AED Skill 1
Scene Assessment

Cycle of Care: AB-CABS™

Continue Until Help or AED Arrives

C Chest Compressions

A Airway Open

B Breathing for Patient

S Serious Bleeding Shock Spinal Injury

A Airway Open?

B Breathing Normally?

Assess Scene
Apply Barriers
Airway Open?

Your Goal

Demonstrate the procedures for assessing an emergency scene for safety.

How It's Done

1 STOP – Assess Scene

▲ Ask yourself – What caused the injury?

▲ Are there any hazards? Look for potential hazards such as leaking gas, chemicals, radiation, downed electrical lines, fire, firearms, the possibility of explosion, oxygen depletion, etc.

▲ Can you make a safe approach? Consider how to make a safe approach. Be alert for possible dangers, such as oncoming traffic. Do you need to turn off a car's engine?

▲ Apply barriers as appropriate and if available.

2 THINK – Formulate Safe Action Plan

▲ Can you remain safe while helping? Remember that your safety must be the first priority. Know your limitations.

▲ What emergency care may be needed?

▲ How can you activate local EMS?

▲ Think about your training and relax.

3 ACT – Begin Providing Care

▲ Follow the emergency care guidelines you will learn in upcoming skills.

▲ Continue to consider your safety as you provide care.

TRY IT In your practice group, work through the scene assessment steps for the scenarios on the next page. Use steps 1-3 – STOP, THINK and ACT – to assess the scene and form an action plan.

Scene Assessment Scenario Two

Scene Assessment Scenario Four

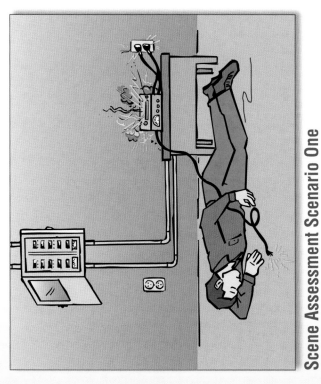

Scene Assessment Scenario One

Scene Assessment Scenario Three

CPR & AED Skill 2
Primary Assessment – Airway Open? Breathing Normally?

Performance Requirements

Demonstrate how to:

▲ Perform an adult, child and infant responsiveness check.

▲ Check for an open airway using one of two methods: head tilt-chin lift or pistol grip lift.

▲ Check for normal breathing.

▲ Perform a Primary Assessment on an unresponsive patient.

How It's Done

1 Assess the scene for safety. Check the adult or child for responsiveness by giving the Responder Statement: *Hello? My Name is _____. I'm an Emergency Responder: May I help you?* If no response to your statement, then tap the patient on collarbone and ask, *Are you okay? Are you okay?* The collarbone is sensitive and tapping it will reveal a level of responsiveness.

▲ With an infant, check responsiveness by pinching or tapping the child. Also, shout his name.

Check for Normal Breathing

Check Responsiveness

Key Points

◆ Use the *Cycle of Care* graphic and the memory word AB-CABS to help you conduct a Primary Assessment.

◆ Deliver the Responder Statement and tap collarbone to check for adult or child responsiveness. With infants simply pinch or tap the infant, along with shouting his name.

◆ Check for normal breathing. If the patient is not breathing or is only gasping, then he needs CPR.

◆ Avoid delaying emergency care by not taking the time to locate and put on barriers.

◆ After establishing patient unresponsiveness, and identifying that he is not breathing normally, ask a bystander to call EMS and secure an AED if possible.

2 Quickly check for an open Airway and normal Breathing. If you are unsure if the patient's airway is open or if he is breathing normally:

▲ Open his airway using either the *head tilt-chin lift* or *pistol grip lift* techniques.

▲ Quickly check for normal breathing. Look for chest movement and listen for breathing sounds. Feel for expired air on your cheek.

▲ This check for normal breathing must be accomplished quickly. If the patient is not breathing normally, he needs CPR immediately.

In an unresponsive patient, the tongue often falls back and blocks the airway.

Use the head tilt-chin lift to open a blocked airway.

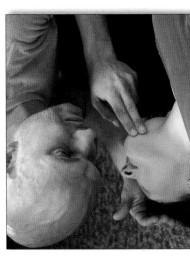

Checking for normal breathing using the head tilt-chin lift.

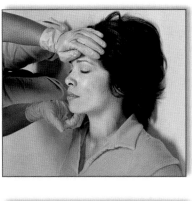

Step Two

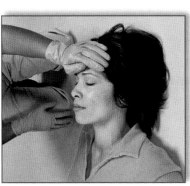

Step One

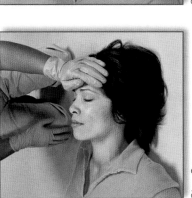

Quickly check for normal breathing.

Open Airway

Head Tilt-Chin Lift

One hand is placed on the forehead or the top of the head. The other hand is used to provide Chin Lift. The head (NOT the neck) is tilted backwards. It is important to avoid excessive force, especially where neck injury is suspected. The chin can be held up by the rescuer's thumb and fingers in order to open the mouth and pull the tongue and soft tissues away from the back of the throat.

Pistol Grip Lift

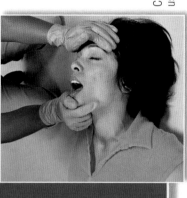

- ◆ With your thumb and index finger, point it like a pretend handgun.

- ◆ Place your thumb and index finger together, as if you "fired" the gun.

- ◆ Place your thumb and index finger along the patient's jaw line. Your thumb is just below the patient's lip and your index finger is positioned across the patient's chin.

- ◆ Use your thumb, index finger and middle fingers to open the patient's lips and mouth. Keep other fingers off the soft tissue of the neck.

- ◆ Place your other hand on the patient's forehead.

- ◆ Gently lift the patient's jaw with your middle finger and tilt head back.

Checking for normal breathing using the pistol grip lift.

3   If the patient is not responsive or breathing normally, ask a bystander to call EMS and secure an AED if possible. If you are alone, use your mobile phone to call EMS. If you do not have a mobile phone, leave the patient to call EMS if no other option exists. This is the *Call First* approach to emergency care. You *Call First* to activate Emergency Medical Services, then you provide assistance.

4   Put on barriers if immediately at hand. Do not delay emergency care if barriers are absent.

5   If the patient is unresponsive and not breathing normally, immediately begin giving CPR. (You will learn CPR in the next few skills. DO NOT PRACTICE CPR ON ANOTHER PARTICIPANT.)

TRY IT

In your practice group perform a Primary Assessment on an unresponsive patient who is not breathing normally. If an infant mannequin is available, practice conducting a Primary Assessment on the infant. One person is the guide, reading the steps; one is the patient, while the other is the Emergency Responder. Everyone should have the chance to act as the Emergency Responder. Alter circumstances as directed by your instructor.

Unresponsive and not breathing normally? First call for help, then perform CPR.

CPR & AED Skill 3

Adult CPR – Cardiopulmonary Resuscitation Chest Compressions

Your Goals

▶ Perform adult CPR – chest compressions at a rate of 100 to 120 chest compressions per minute and depressing the chest one-third the depth of chest – approximately 5–6 cm/2–2.4 inches.

▶ Minimize interruptions in chest compressions.

Cycle of Care: AB-CABS™

Continue Until Help or AED Arrives

A B
Airway Breathing
Open? Normally?

C Chest Compressions

A Airway Open

B Breathing for Patient

S Serious Bleeding Shock Spinal Injury

Chest Compressions

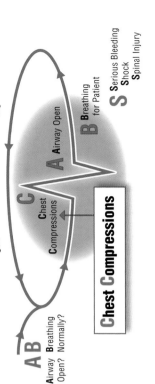

Key Points

◆ CPR is a two-step process. Step one – chest compressions are followed by step two – rescue breathing. During this skill, you'll learn step one.

◆ If you are unable or feel uncomfortable giving a patient the rescue breaths – relax. Give the patient immediate and continuous chest compressions. Chest compressions alone are very beneficial to an unresponsive patient who is not breathing normally. Your efforts will still help circulate blood that contains oxygen.

◆ Use the *Cycle of Care* and AB-CABS memory word to help you remember to perform Chest Compressions before opening a patient's Airway and Breathing for the patient.

◆ Give the Responder Statement and tap the patient on the collarbone. If the patient is unresponsive, quickly check for an open airway and normal breathing.

◆ If the patient is not breathing normally, immediately begin Chest Compressions.

◆ The patient must be on his back and on a sturdy surface prior to beginning chest compressions.

◆ Only practice CPR – chest compressions on a mannequin, never on another participant.

Check Responsiveness

Open Airway

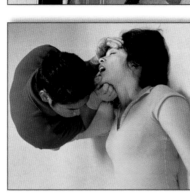
Check for Normal Breathing

Alert EMS

How It's Done

1 Assess the scene for safety. Check the patient for responsiveness by giving the Responder Statement: *Hello? My Name is* _____ . *I'm an Emergency Responder. May I help you?* If no response to your statement, then tap the patient on collarbone and ask, *Are you okay? Are you okay?* The collarbone is sensitive and tapping it will reveal a level of responsiveness.

2 Quickly check for an open Airway and normal Breathing.

> **NOTE** – In the first few minutes after cardiac arrest, a patient may be barely breathing, or taking infrequent, noisy, gasps. This is often termed *agonal breathing* and must not be confused with normal breathing.

3 Alert EMS if the patient is unresponsive and not breathing normally. *Call First* before providing care.

▲ Ask a bystander to call EMS and secure an AED if possible.

▲ If you are alone, use your mobile phone to call EMS.

▲ Leave the patient to call EMS if no other option exists.

Proper Compression Site

Chest Compressions

4 Position patient on his back (if not already in this position).

5 Locate the chest compression site.

▲ Expose the patient's chest only if necessary to find the compression site.

▲ Find the compression site by putting the heel of one hand in the chest center. On some individuals, this position is between the nipples.

▲ Place your other hand on top of the hand already on the chest and interlock your fingers.

▲ Use the palm of your hand on the compression site. Keep fingers off the chest.

6 Deliver chest compressions.

▲ Position yourself so that your shoulders are directly over your hands and your arms are straight – lock your elbows.

▲ Keep the force of the compressions straight down – avoid pushing on the rib cage or the lower tip of the breastbone. With locked elbows, allow your body weight to deliver the compressions.

▲ To provide effective chest compressions you should push hard and push fast, depressing the breast bone approximately one-third the depth of the patient's chest – approximately 5-6 cm/2-2.4 inches.

▲ After each compression, release, allowing the chest to return to its normal position.

▲ Repeat at a pace of – one-two-three-four – and so on, (counting fast) for 30 compressions. Perform the compressions as fluidly as possible. Your rate should be 100 - 120 compressions per minute. The rate is a lot faster than most people think – Push Hard, Push Fast.

TRY IT

In your practice group, perform CPR – chest compressions on a mannequin. One person is the guide, reading the steps, one watches, while the other is the Emergency Responder. First, practice the steps slowly to make sure your hands, arm and body position is appropriate. Next, practice the steps again in real time.

CPR & AED Skill 4
Adult CPR – Cardiopulmonary Resuscitation
Chest Compressions Combined with Rescue Breaths

Cycle of Care: AB-CABS™

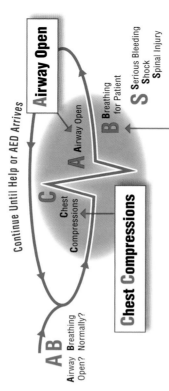

Airway Open

Continue Until Help or AED Arrives

A Airway Open

B Breathing for Patient

S Serious Bleeding Shock Spinal Injury

C Chest Compressions

A Airway Open?
B Breathing Normally?

Breathing For Patient

Chest Compressions

Your Goals

▲ Perform adult complete CPR – chest compressions combined with rescue breathing – at a ratio of 30 chest compressions to 2 rescue breaths.

▲ Minimize interruptions in chest compressions.

Key Points

◆ Use the *Cycle of Care* to help you remember to perform Chest Compressions before opening a patient's Airway and Breathing for the patient.

◆ Give the Responder Statement and tap the patient on the collarbone. If the patient is unresponsive, quickly check for an open airway and normal breathing. If the patient is not breathing normally, immediately begin Chest Compressions.

◆ If immediately available, use gloves and a ventilation barrier to protect yourself and patient from disease transmission. However, do not delay providing emergency care by trying to locate barriers.

◆ Open the patient's airway and pinch the nose closed. Improper positioning of the head tilt-chin lift to open an airway is the number one reason rescue breaths are ineffective.

◆ Effective rescue breaths last just over one second, with just enough air to make the patient's chest rise.

◆ If during an actual situation you are unable or feel uncomfortable giving a non-breathing patient rescue breaths, give the patient continuous chest compressions. Chest compressions alone are very beneficial to a patient without a heartbeat. Your efforts may still help circulate blood that contains some oxygen. Remember – adequate care provided is better than perfect care withheld.

Open Airway

Check Responsiveness

Alert EMS

Check for Normal Breathing

Deliver Chest Compressions

How It's Done

1 Assess the scene for safety. Check the patient for responsiveness by giving the Responder Statement: *Hello? My Name is_____. I'm an Emergency Responder. May I help you? If no* response to your statement, then tap the patient on collarbone and ask, *Are you okay? Are you okay?* The collarbone is sensitive and tapping it will reveal a level of responsiveness.

2 Quickly check for an open Airway and normal Breathing.

3 If the patient is unresponsive and not breathing normally, ask a bystander to call EMS and bring an AED if one is available. If you are alone, use your mobile phone to call EMS. If you do not have a mobile phone, leave the patient to call EMS if no other option exists. This is the *Call First* approach to emergency care. You *Call First* to activate EMS, then you provide assistance.

4 Position patient on his back (if not already in this position).

5 Locate the chest compression site.

▲ Expose the patient's chest only if necessary to find the compression site.

▲ Find the compression site by putting the heel of one hand in the chest center. On some individuals, this position is between the nipples.

▲ Place your other hand on top of the hand already on the chest and interlock your fingers.

▲ Use the palm of your hand on the compression site. Keep fingers off the chest.

6 Deliver chest compressions.

▲ Position yourself so that your shoulders are directly over your hands and your arms are straight – lock your elbows.

▲ Keep the force of the compressions straight down – avoid pushing on the rib cage or the lower tip of the breastbone. Allow your body weight to deliver the compressions.

▲ To provide effective chest compressions you should *push hard and push fast*, depressing the breast bone approximately one-third the depth of the patient's chest – approximately 5-6 cm/2-2.4 inches.

▲ After each chest compression, release the pressure without taking your hands off the patient's chest, allowing the chest to return to its normal position.

▲ Repeat at a pace of – one-two-three-four – and so on, (counting fast) for 30 compressions. Perform the compressions as fluidly as possible. Your rate should be at least 100 - 120 compressions per minute. The rate is a lot faster than most people think – *Push Hard, Push Fast.*

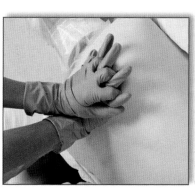

Begin Another Cycle of 30 Chest Compressions

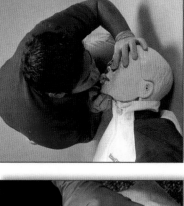

Pocket Mask

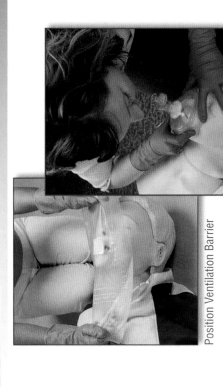

Position Ventilation Barrier

Give Two Rescue Breaths

Open Airway and Pinch Nose Closed

7   Position a ventilation barrier on the mannequin for mouth-to-mouth or mouth-to-mask rescue breaths.

8   Open the patient's airway. Use ONE of two common methods – head tilt-chin lift or pistol grip.

NOTE – If patient has an injury to the face or jaw, gently close the mouth to protect the injured site. While holding the jaw closed, place your mouth over the barrier covering the nose and give rescue breaths through the nose. Certain ventilation barriers (such as a pocket mask) are better for mouth-to-nose than others. Using a pocket mask is another form of rescue breathing called mouth-to-mask.

9   With the patient's head tilted back and the ventilation barrier in place, pinch the nose closed.

10 Now, give two rescue breaths. Each breath should last about one second. Provide the patient with just enough air to make the patient's chest rise. Look for this rise in the patient's chest.

   ▶ If you can't make the patient's chest rise with the first breath, repeat the head tilt-chin lift or pistol grip lift to re-open the airway before attempting another breath. Improperly opening a patient's airway is the most common cause of not being able to inflate a patient's lungs.

NOTE – Do not try more than twice to give rescue breaths that make the chest rise. Minimize delay between chest compressions. After two breaths, whether they make the chest rise or not, begin chest compressions again.

11 After delivering two rescue breaths, immediately begin another cycle of 30 chest compressions. Minimize delays in providing chest compressions.

12 Continue alternating 30 compressions with two breaths until:

   ▶ EMS arrives.
   ▶ You can defibrillate with an AED (Automated External Defibrillator).
   ▶ The patient becomes responsive and begins to breathe normally.
   ▶ Another Emergency Responder takes over CPR efforts.
   ▶ You are too exhausted to continue.

Avoid CPR Fatigue - Alternate Care Between Two Rescuers

NOTE – If more than one Emergency Responder is present consider alternating care. To avoid fatigue, each provider can deliver CPR for two minutes and then switch. While switching providers, minimize chest compression interruptions.

NOTE – If the patient's problem could be a drowning or other respiratory problem, give *Care First*. This means that you provide CPR to the patient for a *short time* and THEN call EMS.

Two national guidelines define providing *Care First* for a *short time* differently. In North, South and Central America, Asia and the Pacific Island countries (AHA Guidelines), it's defined as providing care for approximately two minutes; the European Resuscitation Council guidelines defines a *short time* as one minute.

TRY IT   In your practice groups, perform CPR – chest compressions combined with rescue breathing on a mannequin. One person is the guide, reading the steps, one watches, while the other is the Emergency Responder. First, practice the steps slowly to make sure your hands, arm and body position is appropriate. Next, practice the steps again in real time.

CPR & AED Skill 5
Adult CPR and AED Use

Performance Requirements

Demonstrate how to:

▲ Use an Automated External Defibrillator (AED) on a mannequin according to the machine's manufacturer guidelines.

▲ Place AED pads on a mannequin.

▲ Deliver CPR during AED retrieval, set up and use while minimizing interruptions to chest compressions.

▲ Assist a patient who has been successfully defibrillated with an AED.

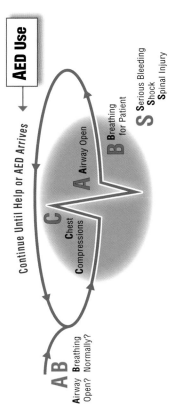

Cycle of Care: AB-CABS™

Continue Until Help or AED Arrives → **AED Use**

C Chest Compressions

A Airway Open

B Breathing for Patient

S Serious Bleeding / Shock / Spinal Injury

A B Airway Open? Breathing Normally?

Key Points

◆ An AED is a sophisticated, battery-powered, microprocessor-based device that incorporates a heart rhythm analysis and a shock advisory system. AEDs are specifically designed for lay rescuers like you.

◆ The AED connects to the patient via two adhesive chest pads. It analyzes a patient's heart rhythm automatically and detects when a shock is needed to restore a normal heart rhythm.

◆ AEDs may be stored with adult pads connected to the AED. Never use pediatric pads on an adult.

◆ In some regions, AED use by laypersons may be restricted. Your instructor will advise you of local protocols.

◆ Remember to stop, think, then act – assess the scene and alert EMS. When available, ask a bystander to call EMS and locate an AED.

◆ Protect yourself and patient from disease transmission by using gloves and ventilation barriers if available. Do not delay emergency care if barriers are not available.

◆ Perform a patient responsiveness check by giving the Responder Statement, and if no response, tap patient on collarbone.

◆ Perform a primary assessment and use the Cycle of Care to continually monitor a patient's medical status.

◆ Whenever possible, CPR should be performed while an AED is located and readied for use. If an AED is immediately available, use it and follow the device's prompts specific to CPR delivery. Use an AED as soon as it's available.

◆ To minimize interruptions in chest compressions, if there is more than one rescuer present, continue CPR while the AED is switched on and the pads are being placed on the patient by the second rescuer.

◆ Pad-to-skin contact is very important for successful defibrillation. If necessary shave the patient's chest hair where pads are placed.

◆ If a patient's chest is wet or sweaty, dry it before applying the AED pads. This will allow for better pad adhesion.

◆ Never place AED pads over pacemakers – place them between two to eight centimetres/one to three inches away. Follow all manufacturer instructions.

◆ Do not place AED pads directly on top of a bandage or transdermal medication patch. These should always be removed and the skin wiped dry before placing pads on the skin.

Key Points

◆ You can defibrillate on a wet surface as long as all safety rules are observed and manufacturer's instructions followed. Your instructor will guide you relative to the specific AED you'll use in the course.

◆ You can defibrillate on a metal surface as long as all safety rules are observed and manufacturer's instructions followed. Your instructor will guide you relative to the specific AED you'll use in the course.

How It's Done

NOTE – The following overview provides you with a generic and universal procedure used by most AEDs. AEDs manufactured by different companies operate differently. Your instructor will guide you on the specifics of the AED used in your course. When confronted with an unfamiliar AED model, refer to the manufacturer guidelines and instructions prior to needing the AED during an actual medical emergency. Even if you find yourself having to use an unfamiliar AED model, don't worry. Most are intuitive and very easy to use. AEDs are simple to operate because they have voice and visual prompts to assist you with set up and treatment of a patient in need.

1 Use the *Cycle of Care* to continually monitor the patient's medical status.

2 If the patient is unresponsive and not breathing normally call EMS. Next:

▲ If a bystander can go get an AED, direct them to do so while you begin CPR. Once the person arrives with the AED, have them set it up and place the chest pads on the patient while you continue CPR. This minimizes interruptions to chest compressions.

▲ If you are alone and know where to find an AED close by, leave the patient to quickly secure the AED.

3 Position the AED close to the patient on the same side as you, the rescuer.

4 Turn AED power ON – follow device prompts exactly.

5 Bare the patient's chest. If the patient is wet, consider quickly drying the chest prior to pad placement. It is not uncommon for a razor to be included with an AED. If available, use it quickly to shave excessive body hair where the pads will be placed.

Bystander brings AED.

Turn on AED.

Call EMS.

Position AED close to patient's ear.

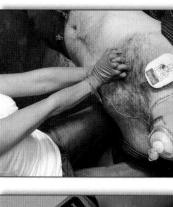

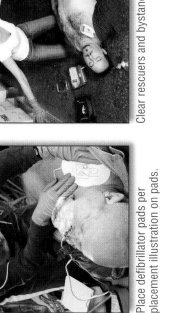

Place defibrillator pads per placement illustration on pads.

Clear rescuers and bystanders.

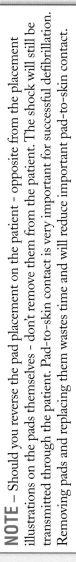

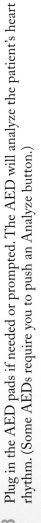

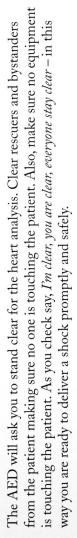

Provide a Shock

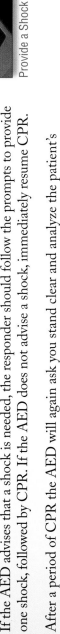

Resume CPR

6　Remove defibrillator pads from packaging – peel away any protective plastic backing from the adhesive pads.

7　As directed by the AED, place defibrillator pads on the patient's bare chest, adhesive side down. Pad placement should follow the manufacturer's illustrations on pad packaging or the pads themselves. Typically:

▲　One pad goes on the upper-right side of the chest, below the collarbone and next to the breastbone.

▲　One pad goes on the lower-left side of the chest, to the left and below the nipple line.

NOTE – Should you reverse the pad placement on the patient – opposite from the placement illustrations on the pads themselves – don't remove them from the patient. The shock will still be transmitted through the patient. Pad-to-skin contact is very important for successful defibrillation. Removing pads and replacing them wastes time and will reduce important pad-to-skin contact.

8　Plug in the AED pads if needed or prompted. The AED will analyze the patient's heart rhythm. (Some AEDs require you to push an Analyze button.)

9　The AED will ask you to stand clear for the heart analysis. Clear rescuers and bystanders from the patient making sure no one is touching the patient. Also, make sure no equipment is touching the patient. As you check say, *I'm clear, you are clear, everyone stay clear* – in this way you are ready to deliver a shock promptly and safely.

10　If the AED advises that a shock is needed, the responder should follow the prompts to provide one shock, followed by CPR. If the AED does not advise a shock, immediately resume CPR.

11　After a period of CPR the AED will again ask you stand clear and analyze the patient's heart rhythm. If normal breathing is still absent, the AED may prompt you to deliver another shock. Most AEDs will wait two minutes before analyzing and shocking the patient again. During that time, continue CPR.

12　As prompted, continue to give single shocks combined with CPR until you see signs of life, are relieved by EMS personnel, or you are physically unable to continue. Signs of life include movement, breathing effort or similar. Do not delay CPR after a shock looking for such signs.

TRY IT　In your practice group, place AED pads on a mannequin and proceed through the Analyze and Shock steps. One person is the guide, reading the steps, one watches, while the other is the Emergency Responder. Each Emergency Responder should:

●　Practice AED pad placement.

●　Practice on an AED Trainer or simulate the steps for analyzing and shocking a patient (mannequin).

Make sure everyone has the chance to act as the Emergency Responder. Alter circumstances as directed by your instructor.

CPR & AED Skill 6
Child CPR and AED Use

Performance Requirements

Demonstrate how to:

▲ Perform complete CPR for a child – chest compressions combined with rescue breathing – at a ratio of 30 chest compressions to 2 rescue breaths.

▲ Minimize interruptions in chest compressions.

▲ Use an Automated External Defibrillator (AED) on a mannequin according to the manufacturer's guidelines for use on a child.

▲ Place AED pads on a mannequin.

▲ Deliver CPR during AED retrieval, set up and use to minimize chest compressions.

▲ Assist a child who has been successfully defibrillated with an AED.

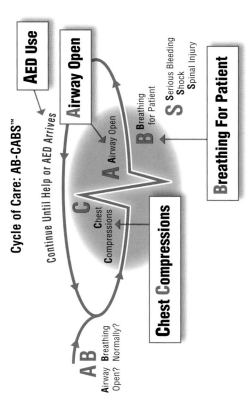

Cycle of Care: AB-CABS™

Continue Until Help or AED Arrives

AED Use

Airway Open

A Airway Open

AB
Airway Open? Breathing Normally?

C Chest Compressions

B Breathing for Patient

S Serious Bleeding Shock Spinal Injury

Chest Compressions

Breathing For Patient

Key Points

◆ A child is defined as an individual between the ages of 1 and 12 years. Regarding this definition, when in doubt about a patient – whether they are a child or an adult – treat the patient as an adult.

◆ Most of the key points from Skill 5: Adult CPR and AED Use apply to children.

◆ When to call EMS:

1. If bystanders are present when you first find a child who is unresponsive and not breathing normally, send them to call EMS and retrieve an AED while you provide CPR.

2. If you are ALONE and no bystanders are present: a) AHA Guidelines – Deliver five sets of 30 chest compressions and two rescue breaths before calling EMS or retrieving an AED; b) ERC Guidelines – Deliver five initial rescue breaths, followed by approximately one minute of CPR before calling EMS or retrieving an AED. c) ARC/NZRC Guidelines do not specify Care First over Call First when a child needs CPR. Provide 1-2 minutes of CPR (chest compressions with rescue breaths) before calling EMS or retrieving an AED.

◆ Often a child's heart stops because of breathing problems and for this reason rescue breaths are very important. However, if during an actual situation you are unable or feel uncomfortable giving a non-breathing child rescue breaths, give the child continuous chest compressions. Chest compressions alone are very beneficial to a child without a heartbeat. Your efforts may still help circulate blood that contains some oxygen. Remember – adequate care provided is better than perfect care withheld.

- Open the child's airway and pinch the nose closed. For very small children you may be able to cover their mouth *and* nose with yours to provide rescue breaths.

- As with adults, effective rescue breaths last just over one second, with just enough air to make the child's chest rise.

- Whenever possible, CPR should be performed while an AED is located and readied for use. If an AED is immediately available, use it and follow the device's prompts specific to CPR delivery. Use an AED as soon as it's available.

- For children between 1 and 8 years old, special child-specific pads should be used or a machine-specific method of reducing the electrical energy delivered by a shock. If a particular AED model does not have special pediatric pads or shock mode, use it as is.

- To minimize interruptions in chest compressions, if there is more than one rescuer present, continue CPR while the AED is switched on and the pads are being placed on the child by the second rescuer.

Checking open airway and for normal breathing.

With small children you may use one hand to deliver chest compressions.

How It's Done

1   Assess the scene for safety. Check the child for responsiveness by giving the Responder Statement: *Hello? My Name is _____. I'm an Emergency Responder. May I help you?* If no response to your statement, then tap the child on collarbone and ask, *Are you okay? Are you okay?* The collarbone is sensitive and tapping it will reveal a level of responsiveness.

2   Quickly check for an open airway and normal breathing.

3   If the child is unresponsive and not breathing normally, have bystanders call EMS if available. NOTE ERC GUIDELINES – At this point, deliver 5 initial rescue breaths before calling EMS or retrieving AED.

4   Place the child on his back (if not already in this position).

5   Locate the chest compression site.

▲   Expose the child's chest if possible to find the compression site.

▲   Find the compression site by putting the heel of one hand on the lower half of the child's breastbone.

▲   With small children you may use one hand to deliver chest compressions. If you can't push the breastbone down approximately one-third the depth of the child's chest or at least 5 centimeters/2 inches, use two hands like adult CPR.

6   Deliver chest compressions.

▲   Position yourself so that you are directly over your hand and your arm is straight – lock your elbow.

▲   Keep the force of the compressions straight down – avoid pushing on the rib cage or the lower tip of the breastbone. Carefully allow your body weight to deliver the compressions.

▲   To provide effective chest compressions you should *push hard* and *push fast*, depressing the breastbone approximately one-third the depth of the child's chest – at least approximately 5 centimeters/2 inches.

▲   After each chest compression, release the pressure without taking your hands off the child's chest, allowing the chest to return to its normal position.

▲   Repeat at a pace of – one-two-three-four – and so on, (counting fast) for 30 compressions. Perform the compressions as fluidly as possible. Your rate should be at least 100 - 120 compressions per minute. The rate is a lot faster than most people think – *Push hard, push fast.*

7   If you feel the need to protect yourself, position a ventilation barrier on the mannequin for mouth-to-mouth or mouth-to-mask rescue breaths.

8   Open the child's airway. Use ONE of two common methods – head tilt-chin lift or pistol grip lift.

9   With the child's head tilted back, pinch the nose closed or cover the nose with your mouth in very small children.

10   Now, take a normal breath yourself and give the child two rescue breaths. Each breath should last about one second. Provide the child with just enough air to make his chest rise. Look for this rise in the child's chest.

▲   If you can't make the child's chest rise with the first breath, repeat the head tilt-chin lift or pistol grip lift to re-open the airway before attempting another breath. Consider looking in the child's mouth for a visible obstruction that can be readily removed.

▲   If you cannot make the child's chest rise with rescue breaths, quickly return to chest compressions. Only attempt 2 rescue breaths.

11   After delivering two rescue breaths, immediately begin another cycle of 30 chest compressions. Minimize delays in providing chest compressions.

Give the child two rescue breaths.

NOTE – The following overview provides you with a generic and universal procedure used by most AEDs. AEDs manufactured by different companies operate differently. Your instructor will guide you on the specifics of the AED used in your course. If a bystander can go and retrieve an AED, direct them to do so while you continue CPR. Once the person arrives with the AED, have them set it up, connect pediatric pads if available, and place the chest pads on the child while you continue CPR. This minimizes interruptions to chest compressions. Use the AED as soon as you have it.

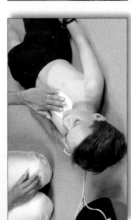
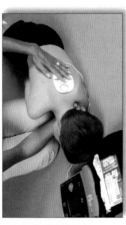

Place defibrillator pads.

If needed, plug in pads.

Clear rescuers and bystanders.

If prompted, push shock button.

12 Position the AED close to the child on the same side as the rescuer.

13 Turn AED power ON – follow device prompts exactly.

14 If the AED has child-specific defibrillator pads, remove them from packaging – peel away any protective plastic backing from the pads.

▲ If child pads are not available, or the AED does not have a child key or switch, use the adult pads or adult settings.

NOTE – For best shock results, some manufacturers illustrate placement of child-specific pads different than adults. They illustrate one pad to be placed on the middle of the child's back between the shoulder blades and the other pad in the middle of the chest.

15 As directed by the manufacturer, place defibrillator pads on child's bare chest, adhesive side down (note placement illustrations on pad packaging or pads).

16 Plug in the AED pads if needed or prompted. AED will analyze the child's heart rhythm. (Some AEDs require you to push an Analyze button.)

17 Clear rescuers and bystanders from the child making sure no one is touching the patient. Also, make sure no equipment is touching the child. Say, *I'm clear, you are clear, everyone is clear.*

18 If the AED advises that a shock is needed, the responder should follow the prompts to provide one shock, followed by CPR. If the AED does not advise a shock, immediately resume CPR.

19 The AED will again analyze the child's heart rhythm. If normal breathing is still absent, the AED may prompt you to deliver another shock. Most AEDs will wait two minutes before analyzing and shocking the child again. During that time, continue CPR.

20 As prompted, continue to give single shocks combined with CPR until the child resumes breathing or until relieved by EMS personnel.

21 If the child begins breathing normally, support the open airway and continue to use the *Cycle of Care* to monitor the child's medical status.

TRY IT

In your practice groups, perform child CPR – chest compressions combined with rescue breathing on a mannequin. Next, practice AED use on a mannequin and proceed through the Analyze and Shock steps. One person is the guide, reading the steps, one watches, while the other is the Emergency Responder. First, practice the steps slowly to make sure your hand, arm and body position is appropriate. Next, practice the steps again in real time. You might also consider having one person continue child CPR while another sets up the AED and places the pads on the mannequin.

CPR & AED Skill 7

Infant CPR

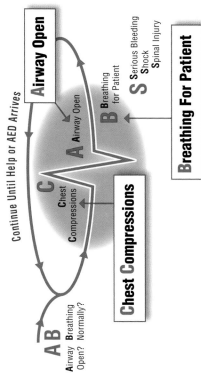

Cycle of Care: AB-CABS™

Continue Until Help or AED Arrives

Airway Open

C Chest Compressions

A Airway Open

B Breathing for Patient

A Airway Open?
B Breathing Normally?

Chest Compressions

S Serious Bleeding
Shock
Spinal Injury

Breathing For Patient

Performance Requirements

Demonstrate how to:

▲ Perform complete CPR for an infant – chest compressions combined with rescue breathing – at a ratio of 30 chest compressions to 2 rescue breaths.

▲ Minimize interruptions in chest compressions.

Key Points

◆ An infant is defined as a baby who is younger than 1 year.

◆ When to call EMS:

  1. If bystanders are present when you first find a child who is unresponsive and not breathing normally, send them to call EMS and retrieve an AED while you provide CPR.

  2. If you are ALONE and no bystanders are present: 1) AHA Guidelines – Deliver five sets of 30 chest compressions and two rescue breaths before calling EMS or retrieving an AED; 2) ERC Guidelines – Deliver five rescue breaths, followed by 1 minute of 30 chest compressions and two rescue breaths before calling EMS or retrieving an AED. 3) ARC/NZRC Guidelines do not specify Care First over Call First when an infant needs CPR. Provide 1-2 minutes of CPR (chest compressions with rescue breaths) before calling EMS or retrieving an AED.

◆ It is very important to provide infants with rescue breaths, along with chest compressions. Often an infant's heart stops because of breathing difficulty or they cannot breathe at all. However, if during an actual situation you are unable or feel uncomfortable giving a non-breathing infant rescue breaths, give the infant continuous chest compressions. Chest compressions alone are very beneficial to an infant without a heartbeat. Your efforts may still help circulate blood that contains some oxygen. Remember – *adequate care provided is better than perfect care withheld.*

◆ As with adults and children, when delivering infant CPR chest compressions, *push hard and push fast.* However, don't be afraid of hurting an infant during chest compressions. With infants it's better to push too hard than not hard enough.

◆ There are case reports demonstrating successful use of AEDs on infants. However, AED use on infants is not supported by definitive research. For this reason AED use by lay Emergency Responders on infants is not recommended.

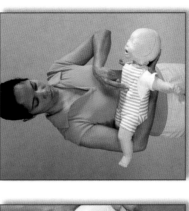

Quickly check for an open airway and normal breathing.

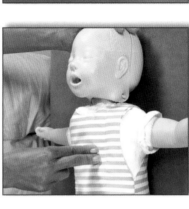

Provide effective chest compressions with two fingers.

How It's Done

1 Assess the scene for safety. If a parent or guardian is present, ask if you may assist the infant.

2 Check the infant for responsiveness by pinching or tapping the infant, along with shouting his name.

3 Quickly check for an open airway and normal breathing.

4 If the infant is unresponsive and not breathing normally, have bystanders call EMS if available. NOTE ERC GUIDELINES - At this point, deliver 5 initial rescue breaths before calling EMS.

5 Place the infant on his back (if not already in this position).

6 Locate the chest compression site.

▲ Expose the infant's chest if possible to find the compression site.

▲ Find the compression site by putting two fingers on the breastbone, just below the nipple line.

7 Deliver chest compressions.

▲ With your two fingers, push straight down on the infant's breastbone.

▲ To provide effective chest compressions you should *push hard and push fast*, depressing the breast bone one-third the depth of the infant's chest or approximately 4 centimeters/1.5 inches.

▲ After each chest compression, release the pressure without taking your fingers off the infant's chest, allowing the chest to return to its normal position.

▲ Repeat at a pace of – one-two-three-four – and so on, (counting fast) for 30 compressions. Perform the compressions as fluidly as possible. Your rate should be at least 100 - 200 compressions per minute. The rate is a lot faster than most people think – *Push hard, push fast.*

8 If you feel the need to protect yourself, position a ventilation barrier on the infant mannequin for mouth-to-mouth or mouth-to-mask rescue breaths.

9 Open the infant's airway. Use ONE of two common methods – head tilt-chin lift or pistol grip lift.

Give rescue breaths.

10 With the infant's airway open, take a breath yourself. Cover the infant's mouth and nose with your mouth. If your mouth is too small, simply put your mouth over the infant's nose and hold his mouth closed to prevent escaping air.

11 Now, give the infant two rescue breaths (with infants rescue breaths are more like "puffs" of air). Each breath should last about one second. Provide the infant with just enough air to make his chest rise. Look for this rise in the infant's chest.

► If you can't make the infant's chest rise with the first breath, repeat the head tilt–chin lift or pistol grip lift to re-open the airway before attempting another breath. Consider looking in the infant's mouth for a visible obstruction that can be readily removed.

► If you cannot make the infant's chest rise with rescue breaths, quickly return to chest compressions. Only attempt 2 rescue breaths.

12 After delivering two rescue breaths, immediately begin another cycle of 30 chest compressions. Minimize delays in providing chest compressions.

13 Continue CPR until the infant resumes breathing or until relieved by EMS personnel.

14 If the infant begins breathing normally, support the open airway and continue to use the *Cycle of Care* to monitor the infant's medical status.

TRY IT   In your practice groups, perform infant CPR – chest compressions combined with rescue breathing on an infant mannequin. One person is the guide, reading the steps, one watches, while the other is the Emergency Responder. First, practice the steps slowly to make sure your finger, arm and body position is appropriate. Next, practice the steps again in real time.

CPR & AED Skill 8
Adult and Child Choking

Performance Requirement

Demonstrate how to assist a conscious (responsive) and unconscious (unresponsive) choking adult and child with a partial or complete (severe) airway obstruction.

Cycle of Care: AB-CABS™

Continue Until Help or AED Arrives

C Chest Compressions

A Airway Open

B Breathing for Patient

S Serious Bleeding Shock Spinal Injury

A B Airway Open? Breathing Normally?

Breathing Normally?

Key Points

- Remember to stop, think, then act.

- If the patient is coughing, wheezing or can speak (partial airway obstruction), observe until the patient expels the obstruction. Reassure and encourage the patient to keep coughing to expel the foreign material. Call EMS if breathing becomes worse.

- Remember that a conscious adult must give consent before you do anything. A head nod is sufficient.

- If the blockage is severe, the patient will not be able to cough, wheeze, speak or make sounds.

- Perform chest thrusts on pregnant or obese patients rather than abdominal thrust (even with obese children).

- Patients who receive the treatment for conscious choking should be medically evaluated to rule out any life-threatening complications.

- The steps for assisting a child who becomes unconscious while choking are different from the steps for assisting an adult who becomes unconscious while choking.

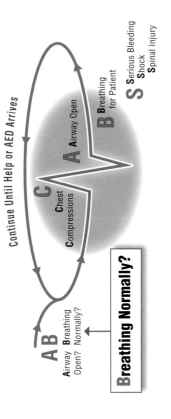

Stand Behind Patient

Locate Navel - Belly Button

Make a Fist

Place Other Hand Over Fist

Bend Arms/Elbows Outward

Perform Inward - Upward Thrusts

Conscious Choking Chest Thrusts

Conscious Choking Adult or Child

How It's Done

AHA Guidelines (North, South and Central America, Asia, regions in Africa, and the Pacific Island countries)

1 Start by asking a responsive adult/child – *"Are you choking?"*

2 If the patient cannot speak or is not breathing normally, give the Responder Statement *"Hello? My name is _____. I'm an Emergency Responder. May I help you?"*

3 When permission is granted (a head nod is sufficient), alert EMS and proceed with attempts to dislodge the object.

4 Consider chest thrusts if abdominal thrusts are not effective. Begin with chest thrusts on adults/children who are pregnant or markedly obese.

Conscious Choking Abdominal Thrusts

1 Stand behind the adult/child and place your arms around waist. You may need to kneel with a small child.

2 Locate the adult/child's navel (belly button) – the thrust site is two finger widths above it.

3 Make a fist and place the thumb side on the thrust site.

4 Place your other hand over the outside of the fist.

5 Bend your arms and elbows outward to avoid squeezing the rib cage.

6 Perform quick inward and upward thrusts until the obstruction is cleared or the adult/child becomes unconscious.

7 Once the obstruction is cleared, encourage the adult/child to breathe and monitor the patient.

Conscious Choking Chest Thrusts

1 Stand behind the adult/child and place your arms around body, under armpits. You may need to kneel with a small child.

2 Follow the lowest rib upward until you reach the point where the ribs meet in the center.

3 Feel the notch on the lower half of the breastbone (sternum) and place your middle and index finger on the notch.
This is the same compression point as for CPR.

4 Make a fist and place the thumb side on the thrust site above your fingers on the notch.

5 Place the other hand over the outside of the fist.

6 Perform quick inward thrusts until the object is expelled or the adult/child becomes unconscious.

7 Avoid putting pressure on the rib cage.

8 Stop if the obstruction clears, encourage the adult/child to breathe and monitor the patient.

How It's Done

Australia and New Zealand (ANZCOR) Guidelines

1 Start by asking a responsive patient – *"Are you choking?"* Assess for effective cough. If effective, reassure and encourage patient to keep coughing.

2 If the patient cannot speak or is not breathing normally, give the Responder Statement *"Hello? My name is _____. I'm an Emergency Responder. May I help you?"*

3 When permission is granted (a head nod is sufficient), alert EMS and proceed with attempts to dislodge the object.

4 Begin with back blows then move to chest thrusts. Alternate back blows with chest thrusts until the obstruction is cleared or the patient becomes unconscious.

Conscious Choking Back Blows

1 To deliver back blows, take a position to the side and slightly behind the patient.

2 Support the chest with one hand, and lean the patient forward.

3 Perform up to five sharp back blows with the heel of one hand in the middle of the back between the shoulder blades.

4 Check to see if each back blow has relieved the airway obstruction. The aim is to relieve the obstruction with each blow rather than to give all five blows.

5 If back blows do not clear the obstruction, switch to chest thrusts.

Conscious Choking Chest Thrusts

1 Stand, sit or kneel behind the patient and place your arms around the body, under the armpits.

2 Identify the same compression point as for CPR and give up to five chest thrusts. These are similar to chest compressions but sharper and delivered at a slower rate.

3 With each chest thrust, check to see whether the airway obstruction has been relieved. The aim is to relieve the obstruction rather than deliver all five chest thrusts.

4 If the obstruction is still not relieved and the patient remains responsive, continue alternating five back blows with five chest thrusts.

5 If the obstruction clears, encourage the patient to breathe and monitor the patient.

6 If the patient becomes unconscious, begin CPR.

How It's Done

European Resuscitation Council Guidelines

1 Start by asking a responsive patient – *"Are you choking?"*

2 If the patient cannot speak or is not breathing normally, give the Responder Statement *"Hello? My name is _____. I'm an Emergency Responder. May I help you?"*

3 When permission is granted (a head nod is sufficient), alert EMS and proceed with attempts to dislodge the object.

4 Begin with back blows then move to abdominal thrusts. Alternate back blows with abdominal thrusts until the obstruction is cleared or the patient becomes unconscious.

Conscious Choking Back Blows

1 To deliver back blows, take a position to the side and slightly behind the patient.

2 Support the chest with one hand, and lean the patient forward.

3 Firmly strike the person between the shoulder blades with the heel of the other hand five times.

4 If five back blows do not clear the obstruction, switch to abdominal thrusts.

5 Stop if the obstruction clears, encourage the patient to breathe and monitor the patient.

Conscious Choking Abdominal Thrusts

1 Stand behind the patient and place both arms round the upper part of the abdomen.

2 Lean the patient forward.

3 Clench your fist and place it between the navel (belly button) and the ribcage.

4 Grasp this hand with your other hand and pull sharply inwards and upwards.

5 Repeat five times.

6 If five abdominal thrusts do not clear the obstruction, switch to back blows.

7 Stop if the obstruction clears, encourage the patient to breathe and monitor the patient.

Look in Mouth – Remove Visible Obstruction

Activate EMS – Begin CPR

Rescue Breaths

Unconscious Choking Adult

1 If a responsive, choking adult becomes unconscious while you are trying to help, carefully help the unconscious adult to the ground.

2 Activate EMS if not already called.

3 Begin CPR as per Skill 4 – Adult CPR: Chest Compressions Combined With Rescue Breaths.

4 Following each set of chest compressions, quickly look in the adult's mouth for objects or obstructions; remove it but do not perform blind finger sweeps because they may push obstructing objects in further, making expulsion more difficult.

5 If no object is seen or the object has been removed, proceed with two rescue breaths.

6 Continue CPR until obstruction is relieved or EMS arrives.

Unconscious Choking Child

1 If a responsive, choking child becomes unconscious while you are trying to help, carefully help the unconscious child to the ground.

2 Yell out for help and assistance.

3 Begin CPR as per Skill 6 – Child CPR and AED Use.

4 Following each set of chest compressions, quickly look in the child's mouth for objects or obstructions; remove it but do not perform blind finger sweeps because they may push obstructing objects in further, making expulsion more difficult.

5 If no object is seen or the object has been removed, proceed with two rescue breaths.

6 Continue CPR – 30 chest compressions follow by two rescue breaths. After five sets of CPR, call EMS and get an AED if close by.

7 Continue CPR until obstruction is relieved or EMS arrives.

TRY IT

In your practice group, perform the steps to assist a conscious choking adult or child. One person is the patient, while the other is the Emergency Responder. Make sure everyone has the chance to act as the Emergency Responder.

Remember – Do not actually perform thrusts on another participant during practice. Next, discuss and/or perform the steps for assisting a child or adult who has become unconscious from a choking incident. Your instructor will direct you. Alter circumstances as directed by your instructor.

CPR & AED Skill 9
Infant Choking

NOTE – This skill is based on the American Heart Association guidelines and required in the regions serviced by EFR Americas when child and infant emergency care skills are taught.

Performance Requirement

Demonstrate how to assist a conscious (responsive) and unconscious (unresponsive) choking infant with a partial or complete (severe) airway obstruction.

Conscious Choking Infant
How It's Done

1 If a parent or guardian is present, give the Responder Statement and ask if you may assist the infant.

2 If available, send someone to alert EMS. If alone, continue assisting the infant.

3 Look in the infant's mouth and carefully remove any visible objects.

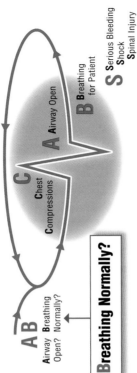
Look in infant's mouth, remove visible objects.

Cycle of Care: AB-CABS™

Continue Until Help or AED Arrives

C Chest Compressions
A Airway Open
B Breathing for Patient
S Serious Bleeding / Shock / Spinal Injury

AB Airway Open? Breathing Normally?

Breathing Normally?

Key Points

◆ Remember to stop, think, then act.

◆ If the infant is coughing, wheezing or crying (partial airway obstruction), observe until the object is expelled by the infant's own efforts. Encourage the infant to keep coughing to expel the foreign material.

◆ Remember to obtain parent/guardian consent before you do anything.

◆ If the obstruction persists for more than a few minutes, stay with the infant and send others to alert EMS or take the infant with you as you call EMS.

◆ Quickly look in the infant's mouth for objects or obstructions; remove it but do not perform blind finger sweeps because they may push obstructing objects in further, making expulsion more difficult.

◆ If the infant becomes unconscious, begin CPR. Chest compressions may help expel the obstruction.

◆ Infants who receive the conscious choking treatment should be medically evaluated to rule out any life-threatening complications.

◆ Do not perform abdominal thrusts on infants as it may damage the relatively large, unprotected liver.

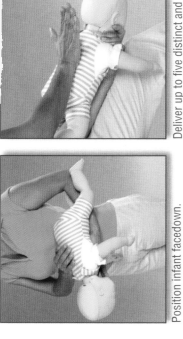

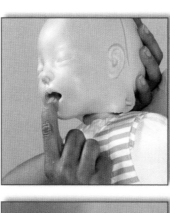

Deliver up to five distinct and separate back blows.

Look in the infant's mouth, remove visible objects.

Position infant facedown.

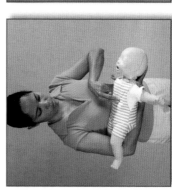

Provide up to five, distinct chest thrusts.

Rescue breaths.

Deliver CPR.

Conscious Choking Back Blows

1 Position infant facedown on your forearm and support the infant's head and neck with your hand.

2 With the infant's head slightly lower than the body, deliver up to five distinct and separate back blows between shoulder blades with heel of your hand. The aim is to relieve the obstruction with each blow rather than to give all five back blows.

3 If the object is not dislodged after five back blows, support infant's head and turn infant over. Keep the infant's spine straight while turning him over.

4 Look in the infant's mouth and carefully remove any visible objects.

Conscious Choking Chest Thrusts

1 To perform chest thrusts, place infant on his back (on rescuer's arm or thigh) with head lower than the body.

2 Locate the chest compression site. This is the same compression site as Infant CPR.

3 Provide up to five, distinct chest thrusts. The aim is to relieve the obstruction with each compression, rather then to deliver all five chest thrusts.

4 Look in the infant's mouth and carefully remove any visible objects.

5 If the object is not dislodged, repeat back blows and chest thrusts. Continue until the object is dislodged and the infant begins to breathe, cry or cough or infant becomes unresponsive.

Unconscious Choking Infant

1 If a responsive, choking infant becomes unconscious while you are trying to help, place the infant on a flat, firm surface. A table or crib will work.

2 Yell out for help and assistance.

3 Begin CPR as per Skill 7 – Infant CPR.

4 Following each set of chest compressions, quickly look in the child's mouth and attempt to remove any visible obstruction. If an object is seen, you should carefully remove the object.

5 If no object is seen or the object has been removed, proceed with two rescue breaths.

6 Continue CPR – 30 chest compressions follow by two rescue breaths. After five sets of CPR, call EMS.

7 Continue CPR until obstruction is relieved or EMS arrives.

TRY IT In your practice group, perform the steps to assist a conscious choking infant using an infant mannequin. Your instructor will direct you. Alter circumstances as directed by your instructor.

Participant Notes

Participant Notes

Participant Notes